THINGS I LEARNED FROM
FROM
MARIO'S BUTT

THINGS I LEARNED FROM MARIO'S BUTT

A SERIES OF GAMING BUTT CRITIQUES

LAURA KATE DALE

ILLUSTRATED BY ZACK FLAVIN

unbound

First published in 2021

Unbound
Level 1, Devonshire House, One Mayfair Place, London W1J 8AJ
www.unbound.com

Text design by carrdesignstudio.com

A CIP record for this book is available from the British Library

ISBN 978-1-78352-890-5 (hardback)
ISBN 978-1-78352-891-2 (ebook)

Printed in Slovenia by DZS grafik d.o.o.

1 3 5 7 9 8 6 4 2

Thank you to everyone who supported the creation of this silly and serious book, either by picking up a copy or sharing the word.

Thank you to all the guests who contributed their time and words to bringing this idea to life.

Thank you, Zack Flavin – your wonderful art is the backbone of this entire project.

Thank you to Jane, for putting up with my long nights spent writing.

And thank you, dear reader, for taking the time to read a book I poured years of my life into creating.

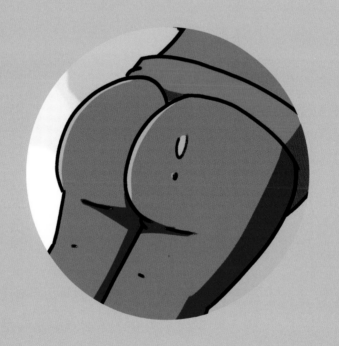

CONTENTS

Prologue...10

The Mario Series...............................12
    Mario...12
    Bowser...12
    Luigi...14
    Donkey Kong.................................14
    Wario...16
    Birdo..16

**Mario & Rabbids: Kingdom Battle –
Rabbid Peach**..................................19

**Katamari Damacy – Prince of All
Cosmos**...20

Lollipop Chainsaw – Juliet Starling......21

Tetris Blocks (Tetris) *by Guest Butt Critic*
Dan Bull..22

Overwatch......................................24
    Tracer...24
    Widowmaker..................................24
    D.Va...26

Undertale..28
    Papyrus *by Guest Butt Critic Brentalfloss*..28
    Asgore..30
    Mettaton.......................................30

Mega Man.......................................32
    Mega Man......................................32
    Mega Man X...................................32

Butts Don't Lie *by Guest Contributor*
Robert Yang....................................34

Mass Effect Interview *with Guest*
Contributor Mark Meer......................35

Mass Effect.....................................37
    Miranda...37
    Uranus..37
    Tali'Zorah......................................38
    Liara T'Soni...................................38
    Krogan..40

Saints Row IV – The President.............41

Skies of Arcadia – Vyse.....................42

The Legend of Zelda.........................44
    Skull Kid..44
    Ganondorf.....................................46
    Tingle...46
    Zelda/Shiek....................................49
    Link...49
    Ghirahim.......................................50
    King Zora.......................................51

Horizon Zero Dawn – Aloy.................52

Rayman – Rayman............................52

SCUM *by Guest Contributor*
Tena Žigmundovac............................54

Beyond Good & Evil..........................56
    Jade...56
    Pey'j..56

The Witcher – Geralt of Rivia..............58

Xenoblade Chronicles 2 – Rex.............58

Halo 60
    Master Chief 60
    Cortana 60

Thomas Was Alone *by Guest Contributor*
Mike Bithell 62

Dead Space – Puker 65

Animal Crossing 66
    Isabelle 66
    Tom Nook 66

Dark Souls 68
    Chosen Undead 68
    Chaos Witch Quelaag 68

Bloodborne 70
    Maneater Boar *by Guest Butt Critic*
        Jim Sterling 70
    A Bloodborne Hunter's Pledge *by*
        Guest Butt Critic Brian Altano 72
    Bloodborne Disc Butt 74

F-Zero – Captain Falcon 74

Pokémon 77
    Spoink 77
    Koffing 77
    Ditto 78

Patrick, The Proctology Training Robot 78

Spider-Man PS4 80
    Spider-Man 80
    Mister Negative 80

Wii 81
    Mii 81
    Wii Fit Trainer 82

The Crash Bandicoot Series – Crash Bandicoot
by Guest Butt Critic Tim Gettys 84

Uncharted – Nathan Drake 87

Tomb Raider – Lara Croft 87

Red Dead Redemption – John Marston 88

Conker's Bad Fur Day 88
    The Great Mighty Poo 88
    Berri *by Guest Butt Critic LittleKuriboh* 90

Minecraft – Steve 92

Dead Rising – Zombies 92

Portal 2 94
    Chell 94
    GLaDOS 94

Dragon Ball Z – Goku *by Guest Butt Critic*
MasakoX 97

Conan Exiles – Player Character 98

**Exploring the Detailed Monster Buttholes
of Conan Exiles** *by Guest Contributor*
Vebjørn Strømmen 100

Banjo-Kazooie – Kazooie 102

Bully – Jimmy Hopkins 102

Street Fighter 105
    Poison 105
    Chun-Li 105

Fatal Fury – Khushnood Butt *by*
Guest Butt Critic Slowbeef 106

Bayonetta – Bayonetta 108

God of War – Kratos 110

Shenmue – Ryo Hazuki 110

Borderlands – Ellie 112

Dizzy – Dizzy 115

Metal Gear Solid Series 116
  Solid Snake *by Guest Butt Critic*
   Max Scoville 116
  Meryl 120
  Johnny Sasaki 120
  Raiden *by Guest Butt Critic Greg Miller* 122
  Hospital Butts 124
  The Science That Supports Solid Snake's
   Nerfed Butt *by Guest Contributor*
   Alanah Pearce 126

Hitman – Agent 47 129

Team Fortress 2 – Soldier 129

Seaman – Seaman *by Guest Butt Critic*
  Justin McElroy 130

Batman: Arkham – Batman 132

Pac-Man – Pac-Man 132

Monster Hunter – Palico 133

Devil May Cry – Dante 133

**Shadow of the Colossus – The Second
  Colossus** 134

Sonic – Sonic the Hedgehog 134

Metroid – Samus Aran 136

Ghosts 'n Goblins – Arthur *by
  Guest Butt Critic Ashens* 138

Nier: Automata – 2B 140

Splatoon – Inkling 140

Yo-kai Watch – Cheeksqueek 142

Duke Nukem – Duke Nukem 142

Final Fantasy XV – Noctis 144

Tony Hawk's Pro Skater – Tony Hawk 146

The Last of Us – Ellie 146

Acknowledgements 147

About the Author and Illustrator 148

Supporters 150

PROLOGUE

When it comes to video-game character designs, one of the most commonly overlooked aspects is the buttocks. Sure, we might see tweets when a game launches about how nice a female character's big arse is, or we might giggle at GIFs of farts from time to time, but how often do we, as lovers of interactive media, stop to really think about the meaning of the butt?

How often do we take some time out of our day to really think about the lore implications of Skull Kid from *Majora's Mask* shaking his booty and what that tells us about his chances of redemption, or Miranda from Mass Effect and the fact that her perfect cheeks are actually a sad reminder of her predestined upbringing? Probably not often enough.

As an author, I have dedicated years of my career to the study of posteriors, from the large to the small, the formless to the toned, and in this book I hope to bring the fruits of that research to you. By the time we're done here, hopefully you should know the difference between a butt that's attractive for attractiveness' sake, and one that's narratively informative, telling us something of worth about the person it belongs to or the world they inhabit.

This is not a book designed to objectify butts and view them solely as sexualised objects; this is a book aimed at learning about what they can teach us about their games, their characters and their worlds. So, without further delay, let's peek behind the curtain and get to the bottom of what makes bottoms so important in video games.

THE MARIO SERIES

Mario

Mario's butt is probably one of the most iconic butts in video games by sheer virtue of how well known he is as a character. Whether you play games or not, the stout plumber in his blue overalls and red cap is familiar far and wide.

Mario as a character is known across the world; he's as instantly recognisable as, say, Mickey Mouse, and will remain so, regardless of the effort put into developing him and his games. This level of automatic notoriety is important to note, because from his butt design alone we can infer that the character of Mario has become sloppy and complacent over the years.

Think back to the original Super Mario: Mario's butt was tiny, barely a few pixels across. He jumped, he leapt, and you never saw his butt as anything of note. However, as the Super Mario series has gone on, his butt has just ballooned in size. First he got more pixels, then he started packing on the polygons, and at this point Mario became known for the flab he carried around the top of his legs.

While this additional posterior fat might be useful – its introduction coincided with his ability to stomp down on things below himself buttocks first – he's done very little to tone his butt or to make interesting mechanical use of it. He's a character who has grown complacent due to the rapid growth of his fame, and the way he has treated his butt is an example of that laxness. It's the flabby, undefined butt of someone who is so famous that he no longer has to make any effort to be noticed.

Bowser

When it comes to Bowser, the big bad of the Mario Universe, we have to take into account the fact that this eternal thief of princesses is not human, and as such what we consider to be his butt is up for debate. Let's say the butt of this reptilian beast comprises any part of the back of his body between his lower torso and his legs. This encompasses the functional parts of the butt but also includes his tail. His tail has to do most of the work that butt cheeks would do on a human, so it seems fair to take it into account when reviewing his rear end.

While we have no direct analogue in the real world for Bowser's species, he appears fairly close in appearance to a turtle. This association with turtles, rather than with any other reptile, is vitally important, due to the sturdiness of their tails.

If we look back to *Mario 64*, we see Mario defeat Bowser in their showdown fights using tail-based combat techniques. Mario uses his superior speed to get behind Bowser, grab him by the tail and swing him around before throwing him directly into spikes. If Bowser had been designed to resemble a lizard instead of a turtle, we would have had a problem, as many lizards can detach their tails when in danger, allowing them to escape their captors. If Bowser's tail had been able to detach, he would have been able to

escape Mario's clutches, been far harder to throw into spikes and might have evaded defeat by the moustachioed plumber.

Beyond that, we can deduce from lore that Bowser has powerful glutes because – and not to be too crude – he has a lot of offspring, and producing so many of them requires a powerful pelvis backed by sturdy buttocks to get the job of baby-making done on a regular basis.

Luigi

Luigi, when compared to his older brother Mario, has an arse defined by its dexterity. Living constantly in the shadow of his more famous sibling and rarely given his own games, Luigi is a character who has to work several orders of magnitude harder than his brother to be noticed, and his butt is the focal point that proves this.

Where Mario can get away with a bland, boring butt that is merely flabby enough for pounding the ground, Luigi has clearly trained long and hard to make sure his butt is chock-full of functional possibilities, making him more capable in a fight than his brother.

If we look at the later entries in the Super Smash Bros. series, from *Melee* onwards, you can see that Luigi wages numerous attacks that make use of his wildly dexterous butt. Perhaps most notable is the attack where he launches himself at enemies, butt first. The sheer momentum caused by throwing his butt sideways is enough to carry his whole body off the ground, causing it to collide with enemies and inflict decent amounts of damage.

While Mario can get away with resting on his laurels, Luigi's backside has been perfectly honed to outshine that of his older and more famous brother. He might have to work a lot harder to get noticed, but he's not afraid to put in the legwork to make his butt work.

Donkey Kong

Not every arse in this world is perfect. Donkey Kong is an example of a character whose rear is poorly designed, at least from a realistically-functional-butt perspective.

Donkey Kong's butt is absolutely miniscule in comparison to the rest of his body. Of course, tiny butts have their place in this world, but DK's bottom is far too small to be a functional centrepiece for an otherwise fabulously large body. For a body like DK's, with a torso and upper body completely rippling in huge furry muscles, you need a central core that supports all that bulk, and this primate is clearly lacking in that department. He's top-heavy and his butt shouldn't be able to support the weight of everything above it; it's just not substantial enough to support all that glory. Donkey Kong seriously needs to do a lot more squats and bulk out that butt or he might just snap under his own weight.

Also, can we just address something quickly? Donkey Kong is an animal, and animals don't normally wear clothing, so why the bright-red tie? It's all about distraction and misdirection. DK knows his butt is not up to scratch, so he tries to draw your attention to his upper body with an eye-catching, out-of-place item of clothing.

Wario

Wario has a rear end that's defined primarily by its size and its utility. We're not just talking about a plump, unrefined butt like Mario's, but a bottom that's practically bulging out of its jeans, and frankly you'd be unlikely to find a tailor in all the land who wouldn't be just a little daunted by the challenge of creating this man's jeans.

Wario's butt is the antithesis to Mario's. Where Mario's butt is an underutilised tool, engaged in thumping but no other actions, Wario makes use of every part and function of his sizeable posterior. In some Super Smash Bros. games he attacks with farts; elsewhere he engages in Luigi-style hip-swing attacks where his rear momentum is the bulk of his attacking power; he jumps to higher platforms via butt propulsion; and he can even use his stored-up gas to create huge powerful mushroom cloud blasts in combat.

It's not a glamorous butt, nor one you'd would want to put your face too close to, but it's a butt used to its fullest potential, achieving things other butts could only dream of. It's a butt that's large not out of complacency, but out of a desire to excel.

Birdo

Birdo, first introduced to Western audiences in *Super Mario Bros. 2*, is a character with infamous origins. Birdo was initially referenced in the game's manual as being a trans-woman, someone assigned male at birth but living as female, something only ever really explored in a Japan-only game called *Captain Rainbow*.

For those unfamiliar with *Captain Rainbow*, the game featured a plotline in which Birdo was arrested by the police for using a women's public bathroom, a clear display of transphobia if ever there's been one, and the player is tasked with finding evidence of her female status to get her freed.

It's not perfect as trans stories goes, with the evidence being used to free her – owning a personal mock phallus – not really proving anything about her female status, but it does show that the character was always intended to be a trans woman. Some may argue that the fact her trans status hasn't been mentioned by Nintendo in the West in twenty years, or in Japan in ten, means she's no longer meant to be a transgender character. Alternatively, you could choose to view this as Nintendo respecting her identity and not bringing up her trans status unnecessarily. Birdo is a woman, and if it's not important to the plot to highlight that she's trans, they'll just address her as a woman.

So, why bring up Birdo's trans status in a book about butts? Well, because oestrogen-based hormone replacement therapy for transgender individuals is known to have a number of effects on the body, one of which is body-fat redistribution. Trans women often find that following hormone replacement therapy they end up with larger, plumper, more rounded and bouncy buttocks as a result of the body relocating its fat. So Birdo's trans hormones have given her a big ol' cute bouncy bottom. You can't argue with science.

MARIO & RABBIDS: KINGDOM BATTLE

Rabbid Peach

Rabbid Peach, one of Ubisoft's Minions-esque Rabbid characters, given a new look and personality as a result of a fusion device let loose on the world, is without a doubt the most memorable of the characters created for this turn-based developer mash-up. From her kiss-my-arse attitude to her perpetual selfie-taking, Rabbid Peach is full to bursting with confidence and charisma.

We know from in-game context that Rabbid Peach is body-positive – she's taking selfies even when in the middle of being swung through the air by a giant, mutant piranha plant – and that body-positivity extends to her buttocks.

When we look at every other Rabbid persona based on a Mario character in *Kingdom Battle*, they wear head-to-toe outfits that match those worn by their real-world counterparts. Rabbid Mario wears overalls, Rabbid Luigi's shirt covers his legs, and Rabbid Yoshi wears a dinosaur onesie.

The only character not to cover their whole body is Rabbid Peach. Princess Peach wears a floor-length dress, but Rabbid Peach only wears a shirt of the same colour and pattern. Why not wear a dress? Because puffy royal dresses hide and disguise buttocks, and if you're loud and proud about your love for your butt, wanting to sneak it into selfies when you can get the angle right, you're better off just wearing a shirt and letting your fluffy butt fly free for the world to see.

Even official statues of Rabbid Peach show her bent in such a way that her butt can get into her trademark selfies; she really wants the world to see that butt, and why wouldn't she? It's a butt fit for the selfie-taking royalty that she is.

KATAMARI DAMACY

Prince of All Cosmos

In *Katamari Damacy* you play a 5-cm-tall prince whose father, King of All Cosmos, has gone on a drunken rampage and consumed pretty much every celestial body in existence. The sky is now barren of stars and planets, so it's your job as the prince to go down to Earth and create new stars and planets from things you find lying around.

In order to do this, you are given a 'katamari', a ball which picks up any objects it rolls over, growing ever larger in the process. The more things you pick up, the more the ball grows, and eventually you offer it to your father to see if it is worthy of being placed up in the night sky.

As the protagonist, the prince, you start the game picking up thumbtacks and dominoes on the ball, plus paper clips and playing cards – all things you can conceivably imagine a 5-cm-tall man could push around the world. However, by the end of the game, you are collecting whole buildings, people, animals, fences, and other objects much larger than you are.

If such an act of physical strength is to be possible, the young prince's form has to be incredibly dense, with a far higher mass per square inch than any creature on Earth. Just think about it: as he pushes a ball made of lamp posts and elephants, his butt is having to do a huge amount of work to keep the momentum going. Not only is the ball heavy, it's made of a bunch of different-shaped objects, giving it an incredibly uneven surface. It's a ball that even a full-size giant would struggle to manoeuvre. That means the prince has one tiny but unimaginably muscular butt.

LOLLIPOP CHAINSAW

Juliet Starling

Juliet Starling, protagonist of *Lollipop Chainsaw*, is a zombie hunter who cut off her boyfriend Nick's head to stop him becoming a zombie, then reanimated the decapitated head and now wears it hanging off her waist while she fights hordes of the undead. Her butt is pretty big, and that's a good thing, because otherwise the boyfriend might have some problems – you know, other than the being-a-decapitated-head thing.

You see, being attached to Juliet's waist, Nick's head spends most of the game bouncing around as she runs around killing zombies, which means his head frequently bangs into her body. So it's a good thing she has a cushioned butt, otherwise Nick would likely sustain some serious injuries before the game is over.

Think of American football, where there's currently a lot of discussion about the need for proper head and helmet cushioning, because without it you risk not just concussion but also long-term brain injuries. The need for padding near where a head is going to be bouncing around is a real safety issue, and one thankfully addressed in *Lollipop Chainsaw*.

TETRIS BLOCKS

(TETRIS)

Have you ever clocked how *Tetris* blocks

Look quite like bottoms with the edges chopped?

This is an odd hot take to share, look, I'm well aware,

But, bear with, I'll break down these quad derrières.

You've got the square one, compact and stocky,

You would call it rotund if it wasn't that blocky.

You've got the one that's long and straight with a waifish waist

That makes it the Kate Moss of basic shapes.

Now take the J-brick (or L if you flip it round),

This one looks a little as if someone's sitting down.

There's the Z- or S-style skewed type of brick,

With a protruding behind that you'd likely describe as 'thicc'.

Then finally the final piece in this squarest dance,

You'll find the T – it just reminds me of a pair of pants.

So yeah, thanks for entertaining my odd hypothesis

and considering how simply shapely every bottom is.

OVERWATCH

🎮 Tracer

The plump backside of Tracer, *Overwatch*'s cover star and time-travelling, magical, lesbian pilot, comes courtesy of an impossibly deep butt crack. In fact, Tracer has a butt crack so deep on her character model that regular humans could not possess similar physiology and survive. Such a crack would inevitably interfere with internal organs and the body's structural integrity.

Most video-game characters with big butts achieve this look by having pre-made shadows painted onto their rear, giving the illusion of shadow – but one that doesn't move or change in response to the lighting. That's not how Tracer's exceptionally deep crack was created, however.

As a result of this bizarrely deep crack, Tracer can be put in literally any pose, under any lighting, and her butt will still cast a shadow implying plumpness and tautness. The way Tracer's bottom is emphasised in any situation is a genuine feat of engineering.

Another aspect of Tracer's butt that plays a big part in its constant visibility is the way her outfit seems either impossibly tight or glued to her arse cheeks. If you look at her bottom head-on, you'll see that rather than finding a natural resting point between the cheeks, the fabric of her costume perfectly follows every contour in a way only achievable with some kind of skin-safe costume glue.

So why was it important that developer Blizzard give Tracer such an exaggerated butt? The answer is evident from the original cinematic trailer for *Overwatch*: Tracer herself is a true butt aficionado.

In the trailer, when Tracer is in combat with Widowmaker, she teleports past the character, then pauses and takes a moment to look back and admire her butt. This isn't a logical or safe thing to do in the heat of battle, so there must be a narrative justification for her action. There is, and it's that Tracer loves butts. She loves them enough to pause and admire Widowmaker's, and she loves them enough to glue her outfit into the deep recesses of her infinitely deep butt crack.

Widowmaker

Widowmaker's butt is one of the most important butts in *Overwatch*, because at least one member of the playable cast feels a glance at it is worth the risk of getting shot.

Widowmaker has a traditionally perfect and flawless butt, and is highly aware of this fact: in most of her character poses she twists her body in awkward ways and painful-looking angles just to ensure her butt is not only seen, but highlighted.

She makes use of her butt as a practical tool, weaponising it to distract her enemies, and Tracer pausing to take a peek shows that this definitely works.

Importantly, not only is the character aware of her butt's perfection, but so are her creators at Blizzard. Widowmaker is given a page more in her official reference art than all the other characters, to focus exclusively on her butt, showing that her perfect posterior is no accident. Blizzard wanted her to have a perfect butt, and one day we should track down the person responsible for it and shake their hand.

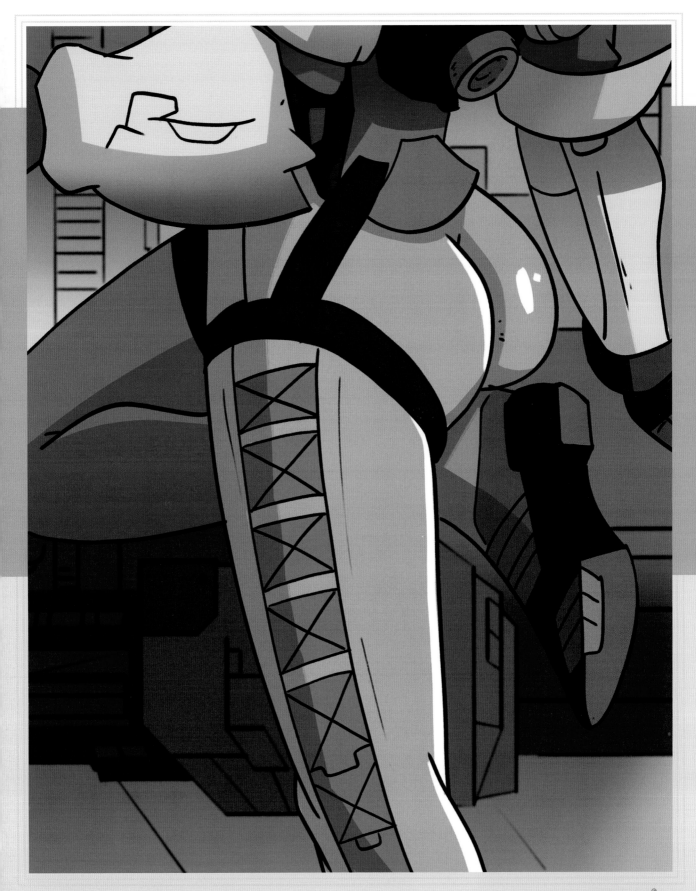

 D.Va

If we look at D.Va's rear end, we see that it's well cushioned and falls within the range of very attainable human butts. The fact it's cushioned makes sense when viewed through the lens of her status as a professional e-sports gamer, in terms of both origin and function.

When sitting for large amounts of time without interruption, as is necessary when training hard for a big upcoming e-sports tournament, you need to be able to remain undistracted by physical discomfort in order to play as effectively as possible. A plump and cushioned rear helps facilitate this; you need a butt that you can simply rely on, and D.Va's certainly fits the bill.

Meanwhile, her status as a professional gamer goes some way to explain her butt type, as sitting for hours, not moving around very much and eating lots of junk food is a recipe for a bit of padding on your bum.

We know that D.Va views her butt's purpose as functional rather than aesthetic. She's not interested in showcasing it; it's just a part of her job. How do we know this? Because her outfit design deliberately makes her butt look smaller. If you look at her legs, the design actually pulls in across the butt, reducing its apparent size. D.Va is more interested in making room on her legs for sponsorship than having her butt look the largest it possibly could, demonstrating that her priorities focus more on her career than her appearance, and that her butt is there to be practical, not for others to ogle.

UNDERTALE

Guest Butt Critic
Brent 'Brentalfloss' Black

Brentalfloss is known for a number of different creative pursuits online. From his video-game-themed comedy songs, presented under the Brentalfloss banner, to developing the comedy party video game Use Your Words, Brent sure knows his video games, and where to find the fun in them.

Brent chatted to us about his favourite butt in video games – or, rather, his favourite lack of butt...

Papyrus

What's in a butt?

OK, that could be phrased better. But really... What makes a butt a butt? Does it require squishiness? Or a crack down the middle? Or even... flesh? No, it actually does not. Why? Because ol' Papyrus shouldn't be denied the right to a butt.

But there is a deeper reason for my argument: he *deserves* a butt.

Yes, Papyrus, the sometimes villain/sometimes good guy of 2015's surprise hit *Undertale*. He's a fan favourite, and with good reason. He's charming even when he comes on too strong, he's funny even when he means to be serious. And he's ultimately well-meaning, even if his long-term goals are spiked with a touch of evil.

Let's talk about Papyrus's anatomy. He's a living skeleton with an oddly geometric skull. It's hard to tell which parts of him are him and which parts are his 'battle body', a partial exoskeleton originally created for a costume party. His chest is protected by a white structure of plate armour which is completed by a flamboyant red cape.

However, his lumbar spine is completely exposed, as are his upper femurs. And then we come to the butt zone. We never see the bony mass that ostensibly comprises his butt because it is contained within a pair of sporty blue briefs. So, visually speaking, his butt might not even occur to players as a thing to consider. However, his butt is the key to his entire character and the root of his confidence.

When you look at Papyrus's life, his interpersonal relationships or his prospects for the future, it can be very hard to see why he would have much self-esteem at all. Strictly speaking, he is not particularly competent. He may be attractive to some creatures, but most human players would not find him physically appealing in the romantic sense. And his professional endeavours seem to fall flat over and over again.

Yet he oozes confidence and projects authority over others. What is it based on? Is it the fact that he's named after the font 'Papyrus', often seen on the awnings of small businesses who didn't hire a logo designer? No! So what is it? Perhaps, rather than needing an actual butt, Papyrus is blessed with a preponderance of Big Butt Energy. It's not his potential worth to others that makes him great; it's his sense of worth in his own eyes!

Who has joie de vivre like Papyrus? Who else makes spaghetti with such gusto? That energy must come from somewhere, and you're probably starting to get a sense of where this might comes from.

To the naked eye, Papyrus is entirely buttless. We may pity his buttlessness as we pity his difficulty making friends or achieving his professional goals. Yet he is undaunted. Despite his apparent shortcomings, he continues to exude the self-possession of a fully butted person. He spends much of the story of *Undertale* chasing recognition and friends. At first glance, that might seem to be a function of loneliness or desperation, but it's more likely that he relentlessly pursues these things not out of a negative sense of lack but rather out of a positive desire to share his Big Butt Energy with others! So see past his near-empty briefs and perceive the butt – that plump, juicy badonkadonk of a rump – that he himself sees.

Asgore

The character Asgore in *Undertale* has two very distinct sides. A big, fluffy, goat-man king reluctantly forced into violence, Asgore would much rather be a calm florist of a man than the violent killer of children he becomes.

Initially a gentle and loving father, the death of his kids at the hands of humanity leads him to feel that the only way to make things right for his people is to kill seven human children, steal their souls and use them to break down the barrier preventing him from waging war on Earth. He does this out of a feeling of obligation, not real desire; he just wants to go back and be with his lost family.

When we look at this big hairy boy's butt, we see a butt of conflict. It's a butt that's toned out of necessity, not passion. He needs to be strong to achieve his aims, but he doesn't love the act of being strong and utilising that power.

It's a toned butt, then, but it's hidden away out of shame. Every time he acknowledges his own toned butt, or lets others see it, it's just a reminder that he's worked hard to go down a path of child-murder that he never wanted. It's a great butt but it reminds him that he's become someone he never wanted to be. This is why he wears a cape and why he wears a series of hanging armour pieces around his waist that cover up and obscure the view of his butt. He has a great arse, but he really wishes he had the soft, squishy, flabby buttocks of a stay-at-home, pie-eating, florist father to two loving kids.

Mettaton

Undertale's sexy resident robot celebrity, Mettaton, is a complex character to butt-review, because his butt can take on multiple physically distinct forms, which each merit discussion on their own terms.

When players first meet Mettaton, he appears in a rectangular boxy form, basically a vending machine with arms and a single wheel. His butt here is not traditionally appealing, with no distinct cheeks and displaying a number of sharp angles which could puncture the skin if touched carelessly. It's cold, hard and with no give, making it difficult to grip.

Once in his EX form, however, Mettaton takes on a far more traditionally humanoid shape. In this flawless, hourglass figure, Mettaton has an arse worthy of celebration, but never turns around to give players a chance to see it. Why? Because he doesn't believe that butts are family-friendly.

At one point in the fight with Mettaton EX, players are asked to tell the robot what they like most about him. If you type arse, butt, or scientific words connected to this body part, such as anus, the fabulous celebrity-bot will inform players that this answer is inappropriate for a family-friendly show. This is a shame, because his butt in this form is truly one the whole family can enjoy.

In his Neo form, his butt remains fabulous but his arse gets handed to him incredibly fast by the player.

It's important to note Mettaton is actually a ghost given a physical container, so while his EX and Neo butts are amazing, they're not inherent to the ghost possessing them. These bodies are described as the ones the ghost had been dreaming of; he wanted a stellar butt, not one suitable for family audiences, and didn't stop until that corporeal butt was granted to him.

In his bodily forms, Mettaton possesses a fantastic arse, but feels that fantastic arses are inappropriate for children's programming. His arse exists, visible through implication and form, always there but never discussed. Just because he wants a perfect body, and perfect butt, doesn't mean he thinks it's okay for us to insist on getting a direct look at it for ourselves. That's fair; sometimes a butt is just for the butt owner to enjoy.

MEGA MAN

▢ Mega Man

When we think about Mega Man as a video-game character, by far his most defining characteristic is his ability to change forms and take on the powers of the many robot masters he defeats. His mechanical body has to be incredibly versatile in order to support this ludicrously high number of configurations, and a big part of this feature depends on the strong build quality of his robot butt.

While Mega Man's butt rarely changes in shape or size itself, the fact it can support so many alternative body configurations is integral to Mega Man's flagship power. As with any sentient being, robot or not, the waist and butt serve a vital role in enabling a bipedal life form to not only hold themselves upright but also move around properly. The glutes support the body in fundamental ways, and when a body can change size or shape at the drop of a hat, a versatile butt is vital. Mega Man's mechanical butt needs to support a variety of different arms and heads, often with different weights, materials, sizes and layouts. Sometimes the layouts are symmetrical, sometimes not, and this wide array of different builds needs a butt which can adapt to shifting needs.

Well done, Doctor Light, you created a mechanical butt that could adapt to any problem it encountered.

Mega Man X

Mega Man X was the first robot created by Doctor Light, and is generally believed in Mega Man lore to be the most powerful robot the Doctor ever created. X was deemed so powerful that he was sealed away for a hundred years to answer ethical dilemmas and ensure that he was only allowed into the world if he was deemed able to use his powers for good.

Given that X is supposed to be superior to Mega Man in every way, it stands to reason that his butt is even better than that of the primary Mega Man. Additionally, thanks to his time spent locked away, he knows the correct ways to ethically use his arse as a powerful weapon. No using this particular arse for war crimes, that's what ethics tests are for.

Mega Man X also avoids one of the key negatives of being frozen for 100 years – butt atrophy – because he's made of metal. He's spent a hundred years learning how best to use his perfect butt, without his butt in any way wasting away. This really is a rock-solid butt.

BUTTS DON'T LIE

Robert Yang

Video-game developer Robert Yang has had a wide and varied career, but is perhaps best known for his series of video games exploring male homosexuality in serious yet light-hearted ways. From *Hurt Me Plenty*, a game about spanking butts and respecting safeword boundaries, to *Stick Shift*, which abstracts a handjob into interactions with a sports car, Robert Yang's games often explore how nudity can be silly, titillating, but also informative and mature.

Here Yang discusses butts and their role in historical carbon dating of interactive art.

Butts talk. Video-game butts, in particular, are total gossips. They'll tell you everything about a game, like when was the game made, or how horny the developers were. Now, there's no such thing as a butt-whisperer (don't be silly, of course butts can't hear you); however, you can totally train yourself to be a skilled butt-listener.

Every video-game butt is a greedy butt. They devour hardware resources on your console or game device, for seemingly little in return. Then why waste valuable processing power on rendering these butts? Like any hungry bottom, a well-crafted video-game butt is always worth it. The butt contains multitudes.

Among the most skilfully crafted butts are 2D, pixel-art renditions; how do you imply a shapely curvature with a handful of pixels? That precious real estate on your screen could be devoted to anything else, and behold, it's devoted to butts. These butts are masterpieces of impressionist painting, expanding in our imaginations far beyond their razor-thin pixel boundaries.

As one of the most notorious gay sex game-makers in the world, I am more familiar with 3D butts. In contrast to 2D butts, these technologically advanced butts seem like fully-realised, delicious voluptuous peaches bursting out of your screen. Yet underneath their ripe, round simplicity, internally in the game engine, these butts are also complex mesh networks honed through decades of military and scientific research.

One of the most straightforward ways to assess a butt is to measure its 'polycount'. By counting the number of 3D polygons in a character's butt, you can roughly assess when a game was made and its working conditions. A relatively jagged butt clearly dates a game to the late 1990s during the PlayStation 1 era, while a full but angular butt points to the early 2000s. It's kind of like radiocarbon dating, except for butts. What might've passed for an impressive butt in *Metal Gear Solid 2* now, decades later, feels blurry and flat, and we can quantify that difference. In this way, every 3D butt harbours a technological decay to be assayed by trained analysts. (In comparison, the classic abstraction of a 2D butt seems timeless. Its flatness is assured, so we move beyond it.)

This is also where it gets complicated. As we enter the 2010s, polycount is no longer a reliable gauge of computational complexity in 3D game art. Instead, we must pay attention to the butt's 'shader', the dynamic rendering algorithm running on the graphics hardware. Does the butt feature advanced 'screen-space subsurface scattering' (SSSS) simulation, or is it a 'raymarched' butt that can easily deform in real-time?

The future of video-game butt technology will bestow behaviour upon the butt, build a butt AI, engineer a butt that literally just won't quit. Indeed, this next generation of butts will capture the ways that butts feel, dance, cry and talk. And, of course, we will listen.

MASS EFFECT INTERVIEW

Mark Meer

Mark Meer is a voice actor, perhaps best known for being the male version of Commander Shepard, the playable protagonist of the original Mass Effect game trilogy. In the series of space exploration games, Commander Shepard travels the galaxy, making alliances and trying to stop an impending extinction-level event.

Mark answered a few questions about Mass Effect butts and revealed some amazing facts, including his favourite butt on the Citadel.

Many aspects of Commander Shepard are customisable by players, but the butt isn't. Is a pre-defined, toned butt important to who the character is?

Mark: While much of Shepard's background and personality are determined by the player, both Jennifer Hale (female Shepard voice actor) and I had certain bedrock elements we could rely on as a foundation for building our performances. These included Shepard's extensive military career and experience as an officer in the field. There are certain aspects of Shepard that are set in stone, and now that you mention it, I suppose one of them is the butt.

At the beginning of *Mass Effect 2*, Commander Shepard gets caught in a large explosion and has to be rebuilt by the human survivalist military group Cerberus. How do you think Shepard felt about his body, butt included, being rebuilt? Does this mean his new butt is owned by Cerberus?

Mark: I would assume that the cybernetic enhancements used to rebuild Shepard included augmentation of the butt, but I'm not sure if said butt was literally labelled 'Property of Cerberus'. As long as it was as good or better than the old butt, Shepard was probably satisfied with the new cyber-butt.

In *Mass Effect 2*, Commander Shepard is known to proclaim that many products or services are his favourite on the Citadel. What do you think was the best butt there?

Mark: Blasto's, without question – though there is some question as to which bit of him is actually his butt.

You've cosplayed Commander Shepard at numerous conventions around the world. Do you feel your butt lives up to the Shepard in-game?

Mark: Fortunately for me, the armour does most of the work, giving me that Shepard shape. Thanks again to David Carpenter for building my N7 armour, including the butt.

MASS EFFECT

⊡ Miranda

First appearing in *Mass Effect 2*, the character of Miranda is designed to be flawlessly beautiful, from her slender figure and blemish-free skin, to her muscle tone and unbelievable large and perky butt.

There's an in-game narrative justification for why her butt needs to be quite so plump. Miranda is the result of parents investing in genetic modification.

Miranda's parents in the Mass Effect series engaged in genetic editing before their daughter was born, with the aim of creating her to be perfect on every level. She's smart, creative, confident, and yes, she has a body that's crafted to be faultless. This is a source of distress for Miranda, as the expectations placed upon her become too much to bear. However much she attempts to escape the fate laid out before her she's unable to completely avoid being reminded that, deep down, she's a science experiment expected to never fail, with the pressure this entails following her forever.

While many may just look at her perfect butt and see something to ogle, a true butt expert looks and sees a tale of impossible expectations placed on a woman who, at the end of the day, is only human. Miranda's butt prevents her from ever truly forgetting that her parents had her whole life laid out before she was born.

Uranus

When it comes to new mechanics introduced in the second Mass Effect game, one of the most memorable – whether you love it or hate it – is the probe-mining tool. *Mass Effect 2* allowed, and somewhat required, players to probe planets for resources, with one planet in particular standing out from the crowd: once you have travelled to Earth's solar system, the game will allow you to probe... Uranus. If you select this option, the ship's AI EDI will tell you to grow up, but you should definitely probe Uranus at least once, just to see if you like it.

OK, easy jokes aside, let's talk about what probing Uranus would really be like. Uranus is an 'ice giant', which most people assume means the planet is just solid ice which you would have to drill into to extract samples. However, that's not actually what the term means. As an ice giant, Uranus was probably cold and rock-solid when it initially formed, but is now in an ethereal state between liquid and gas, being simultaneously both and neither at the same time. Despite what the name suggests, you'd probably be able to grab a handful of Uranus pretty easily without having to drill into it.

There you go: you just learned a few important facts about probing Uranus – and that it's easier and more enjoyable than you think.

Tali'Zorah

One of the Mass Effect series' more visually mysterious alien races, the Quarian are nomads who, after being exiled from their home planet, were forced for many years to exist upon migrant fleets. Due to their weakened immune systems, made more drastically so by years spent in sterile environments, the Quarian have to wear complex suits that keep them protected from pathogens and can be automatically compartmentalised, so if a tear occurs, any infection is isolated to a small area of the body.

In the main Mass Effect trilogy, the Quarian Tali'Zorah works as a technician on the player's ship, repairing mechanical faults and working largely by herself. While Quarian bodies are on average quite humanoid, albeit it slightly smaller and thinner, there's very little we directly see of Tali's butt. What we know about her butt comes largely from context clues.

Tali has lived her whole adult life in a pressurised decontamination suit designed to be airtight against any outside contaminants. One assumes that an airtight suit doesn't vent very effectively, so she likely gets very humid from sweat, particularly with her working a fairly manual job. From this we can surmise that while Tali's butt is probably a small, petite-human butt, it's wrinkly as hell. The same most likely goes for the majority of her species, so whenever you see a Quarian in a Mass Effect game, don't forget that wrinkly prune behind.

Until the day your race can return home and leave your suits, allowing your butts some much-needed fresh air: 'Keelah se'lai'.

Liara T'Soni

Few species in the Mass Effect games are generally considered to be as attractive and mysterious as the Asari. The Asari don't actually look the way we see them in-game; as a species their appearance is shaped by the preferences of the species observing them, and as such every species sees them as having a different look. We play the Mass Effect games as humans, so my comments will be based on our version of their appearance, understanding the limitations that brings with it.

To my taste, Liara T'Soni, the Asari crew member in the original Mass Effect trilogy, appears in those games to have the ideal humanoid butt – large enough to get a good hold of but small enough to be cute, and toned enough to hold a perfect shape.

Or does she? Perhaps Liara's butt, and actually that of any Asari, should be disqualified from best-butts lists because it's impossible for us to get an accurate, objective look at what the butt's appearance actually is. Perhaps, instead, it's the 'ultimate' butt, which wins every competition by default because it appears to be the perfect butt to each and every viewer. It's the infinitely perfect butt, and no one butt can dethrone it.

Even after many years of butt research, this may be the one of toughest questions to be faced with, and the answer still isn't clear. How do you rate an infinite butt?

Krogan

In the Mass Effect games, the Krogan are an alien species who are incredibly powerful combatants and have an incredibly high birth rate. Before intergalactic interference, Krogan women were capable of producing 1,000 fertilised eggs per year, allowing for very fast spread of the species across the galaxy once they had achieved the ability to explore space.

While many space-faring species initially encouraged Krogan space travel to help win wars, others quickly began to fear the sheer numbers of this very powerful race. As a result, a genetically engineered virus called the Genophage was created in order to lower Krogan birth rates so that only 1 in every 1,000 births would survive. This drastically lowered the Krogan population, and its people became insular and violent. Post-Genophage, Krogan tended to worry more about finding things to kill than trying to keep their species alive. They assumed that their extinction was inevitable, and moved forwards as such.

So, what does this have to do with butts? Simply put, without any desire or incentive to attract mates or romantic partners, the Krogan just sort of gave up on even trying to be appealing. Over generations, they focused on combat skill rather than appearance, leading to a species with a tapered, thin waist and next to no butt to speak of. They have a tail on the butt to maintain their balance since they are top-heavy, but the butt itself isn't impressive because it simply doesn't have to be. There's no having to stand out from other Krogan in the dating pool.

Still, there is hope. In one possible ending for *Mass Effect 3*, players can choose to cure the Genophage. If this happens, it is possible that one day, just maybe, we might get to see what a good, high-quality Krogan arse looks like.

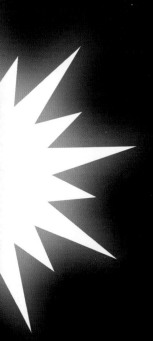

SAINTS ROW IV

The President

Saints Row IV is an absolutely ludicrous game, with an opening sequence where you disarm a nuclear missile while riding it into the air (to a Bon Jovi soundtrack) before leaping off it and landing in the White House, where you become the new president.

Saints Row IV allows players to create their own character, who becomes the new alien-fighting, gun-carrying president of the United States, and a big part of that is deciding how your character should dress.

Now, *Saints Row IV* doesn't actually let you see your character's unclothed buttocks, but it does allow you – in the canon of the game world – to show off the president's butt to the citizens of the USA. You can run around in just your underwear and see your butt in pretty fantastic detail, but taking off your underwear brings a pixelation filter to the image.

Still, being able to see the butt in underwear, then make it translate to seeing the president running around naked, is enough. We know that it is incredibly difficult to arrest a sitting president, so we should just enjoy the political implications of the current president's nudity. Presumably there are people all across the nation calling for the president to be arrested for indecent exposure, but it's just not possible to stop a naked president from attending to their naked business.

SKIES OF ARCADIA

🎮 Vyse

The character Vyse from *Skies of Arcadia* is an interesting character to try and butt review, because it took some serious investigation to work out that his name was in some way connected to his butt.

The name Vyse, pronounced like 'vice', initially seems to be a reference to the idea of immoral behaviour, a poorly controlled behaviour – that kind of a vice. He's a pirate, sure, which would suggest that reading of the name, but he's much more of a positive, spirited Robin Hood-style figure, leading me to believe that perhaps this was not the correct reading of the name. No, in fact the name Vyse is a reference to the character's vice-like tight buns. Yes, it's actually a reference to that metal screw-to-hold-things-together tool.

Why do I feel this? Well, multiple things about his character design, as well as the design of the camera system in the game, lead to the conclusion that his butt is very important.

Firstly, in combat, you can set the camera to loop around the active character. When you do, it comes around high and wide at the front, but low and close at the back. Why else would it do this, if not to better show an up close and personal look at that butt?

Additionally, the way Vyse's butt is treated in other games says a lot about the power of his backside and about the way developers view that power in cameo roles. Vyse has a butt that won't quit, being rereleased on the GameCube and getting cameos in Valkyria Chronicles and *Sonic & All-Stars Racing Transformed*. In Valkyria Chronicles his butt is under a full-body baggy jumpsuit, which I believe is out of fear that his superb cheeks would be a distraction from the main characters in the game. The designers didn't want a cameo taking all the glory.

In *Sonic & All-Stars Racing Transformed* he is allowed to have his butt out, mainly because he is usually sitting down, minimising his level of distraction.

As a side note, Vyse is voiced by Craig Smith in Valkyria Chronicles, the current voice of Sonic the Hedgehog, who also has a very toned arse. Is Craig Smith only willing to voice characters with good butts, perhaps?

Thank you to Pick-a-Butt supporter Stephen Juby for selecting this character to appear in the book

THE LEGEND OF ZELDA
The Legend of Zelda: Majora's Mask

Skull Kid

In *The Legend of Zelda: Majora's Mask*, the primary antagonist is a character called the Skull Kid. Emboldened by the dark magic of an evil mask, this impish child of the forest spends three days trying to cause the moon to crash into the Earth, with the intention of destroying all life on our planet. However, despite these dark intentions, Skull Kid is ultimately a sad, scared child, and one of the key ways we learn about this, early in the game, is via his butt.

To detail a little of the Skull Kid's story, a lot of his anger, resentment and misery are fuelled by loneliness. Once befriended by a group of giants, when the giants had to leave the world, awaiting a time they would be needed, the Skull Kid felt betrayed and abandoned. This is drawn out by the dark mask he wears, which offers him power and fuels his angry thoughts, but it's not all there is of the character: at heart he is still just a child who wants to play and have fun.

When the hero of the game, Link, first reaches the game's observatory, it's possible to spot the Skull Kid standing atop a large tower. When he notices you've spotted him, he turns around and shakes his bottom at you before running away. This simple action is hugely telling, because it demonstrates early on to the player that Skull Kid is still childish and immature, and that he is still ultimately a kid at heart. Seeing this is important as it's one of the few early indicators that there is hope for redemption for the character, and that perhaps he's not a villain who needs to be killed or imprisoned for life in some sort of prison dimension.

When the game ends, and Skull Kid is eventually freed from the mask's control, remembering that butt-wiggle is why we can feel comfortable trusting him to go back into the world without causing any more harm.

Ganondorf

When he is the humanoid character known as Ganondorf, this character's butt isn't anything too special to look at. It's toned enough, it's not abnormally small, it's not too hard to hold, but it's just a very average butt – an everyman's butt, a butt that any of us could possess. This makes some in-universe sense, as Ganondorf is a member of the Gerudo tribe, warrior women to whom only one male is born every hundred years, and Ganondorf is one such male. Much like the Krogan species, Ganondorf doesn't need a great butt to attract women; as the only man in his tribe, it's not like he has to compete with many other men in the dating pool.

However, Ganondorf's rather ordinary butt takes a very different form when he turns into Ganon, the gigantic pig demon that embodies him at his most powerful and dangerous. The difference between the two rear ends tells us some really interesting things about the role of that body part in Ganondorf's attempts to conquer the world.

While Ganondorf's butt is merely run of the mill, Ganon's pig butt is one huge arse, an arse that's impossible to ignore and impossible to forget. If you walked into a party with Ganon, you wouldn't be able to help but notice his butt due to its ludicrous size.

So, here's my theory: Ganondorf transforms into Ganon because of the abilities granted to him by the Triforce of Power, one of the three sacred triangles of the goddess. As it's the Triforce of Power that grants him this transformation, which turns his average arse into a gigantic unforgettable one, we can only conclude that Ganondorf's butt is the source of his power. The larger his butt, the more powerful he is. He holds all of his power in his butt, and that's how it should be – the butt is a place of great importance, and we would all do well to respect the danger posed by a well-wielded behind.

Tingle

Much like our earlier discussion of Super Mario's brother, Luigi, Tingle's butt is another story of a character living in the shadows. Tingle is a superfan of *Zelda's* Link, dressing up like him, wanting to be him and dreaming of being the kind of hero that our protagonist seems to be with ease.

While you'd expect a superfan to mimic their idol's outfit to the letter, Tingle doesn't make any effort to make his outfit a 100-per-cent-accurate replica, and there is a good reason for that.

If you compare Link's and Tingle's outfits, the primary difference is that Tingle wears bright red underwear on the outside of his clothing. Why? Because he's trying to highlight his butt, one of the few areas where he trumps his hero. However functionally smart and cute Link's butt is, you have to admit it is small. Tingle's, on the other hand, is plump, grand, squeezable, and perfectly bubbly. It's one of the few areas where the student can outdo the master, and as such Tingle makes sure that everyone gets a good hard look at it.

Also, when, like Tingle, you float around all day on balloons that have to be popped any time you have a customer, sending you crashing to the ground, you'd better have a cushioned rear to break your fall.

Zelda/Shiek

In *The Legend of Zelda: Ocarina of Time*, a key part of the plot centres around Princess Zelda living hidden away from the world. As one of the three wielders of the sacred triangles of the Triforce, she is being hunted down by Ganondorf and needs to stay under the radar. To complicate things, Link spends seven years in a weird alternate-dimension void, and upon returning to the world is unaware of the seven years of changes to the land. As a result, Zelda feels the need to act as a guide of sorts, shepherding him through the world and helping him to achieve his goals.

So, how do you help a legendary hero to find his way through the apocalypse but stay hidden from an evil wizard? Well, you disguise yourself as the masculine-presenting ninja Shiek.

As Shiek, Princess Zelda unwittingly gives us the best possible look at her buttocks. In nearly every other incarnation she wears big, flowing dresses befitting of a member of the royal family, giving us minimal chance to even speculate about her posterior, but when she's clad in tight-fitting ninja gear, you get a pretty solid look at what this princess is packing back there.

Shiek, or Zelda if you prefer, has a pretty small backside, which tells us a lot about her personality and the type of ruler she is over her nation.

She's clearly not an athletic princess; it's not a toned and defined bottom. This is not the bottom of a princess out battling in wars, on the front line with her troops. However, the fact that her butt isn't plump either suggests that she's not simply lazing around being waited on hand and foot. She's up and about, doing things on the daily; it's just that she doesn't have a medieval treadmill installed in her castle.

Also, it's a good thing for her sake that she's not more curvaceous in the rear, or her disguise would have been more difficult to pull off. Her relatively flat posterior and its lack of overt shape makes her rear less memorable, less open to scrutiny, and makes it less likely that someone will code her as female at a glance. This allows her to travel more efficiently around the land while not being caught out as the princess that the dark lord seeks.

Link

It's really difficult to get a good proper look at Link's posterior. In pretty much every incarnation, every outfit design, every iteration, Link wears a tunic which is just long enough to make it tough to get a decent view of his buns. The fact that his tunic doesn't stick out much from his body implies that Link's butt isn't very large.

However, as an adventurer, he runs and walks great distances, so we can deduce that he most likely has a runner's butt: a small but toned arse, one that's fit for purpose, muscled up from miles and miles of running, with all the fat trimmed away. It's a small butt, a functional, no-frills butt.

These suspicions about Link's butt are ultimately confirmed in *The Legend of Zelda: Breath of the Wild*, where Link is able to be placed in custom outfits, one of which involves Link wearing a pair of tight leggings; as theorised for decades, his butt is indeed a small and functional runner's butt.

It seems fitting that a man with such a small arse would inherit the Triforce of Courage, because his story shows us that, with courage, a small butt doesn't have to hold you back in life.

The Legend of Zelda: Skyward Sword

Ghirahim

A recurring boss in *Skyward Sword*, Demon Lord Ghirahim, is one of the Zelda series' most enjoyable boss encounters. He's not necessarily enjoyable for his mechanics in combat – he's a guy with a sword and some magical projectiles – but he's entertaining in personality and presentation.

Ghirahim is a flamboyant man with a dexterous, lengthy tongue, starkly asymmetrical bob-style haircut and the confidence to rock a male Lycra bodysuit that leaves little to the imagination, including his butt. A rarity in the Zelda series, Ghirahim is a character who not only has a visible butt, but also acts like he's keen for the audience to see it.

Ghirahim's whole deal in *Skyward Sword* is unsettling, unnerving confidence, the kind of confidence that leaves even the strongest of warriors unsure how to proceed. From popping up behind Link and wiggling his tongue near his ears, to walking into scenes with his arms up in a victory pose, he's a character defined by the way he so often acts like he proudly owns the room. He's Ghirahim, and he doesn't care what anyone thinks about it.

Ghirahim's personality, his indifference to anyone's opinion, is why he's the only character in the Zelda series whose butt we get a proper look at. He wears a skin-tight bodysuit because he's a character with nothing to hide, who cares not if you see his rear.

Here's the thing: Ghirahim's butt is undeniably gorgeous. It has plump round cheeks, taught and firm, perfectly proportioned to his frame, without being too large and drawing attention from the rest of his fabulous form.

It's a butt that's instantly recognisable, and it's a little intimidating – *Damn, that's a nice butt*; it makes you feel flustered and thrown off balance, and that feeling of not being in control is exactly what Ghirahim counts on when he's up against a foe. He owns the room, and his enemy is on the back foot from moment one.

The Legend of Zelda: Ocarina of Time
King Zora

In *The Legend of Zelda: Ocarina of Time*, King Zora's butt is one of the few in the game that no player – butt enthusiast or not – can miss.

King Zora is a very large, very heavy, humanoid fish-man who resides in Zora's Domain. Put simply, his butt is very wide, large enough to prevent you passing through a gate to the third dungeon in the game. Seriously, he's just sitting there, upset about his daughter's disappearance, and until you sort out that problem you're not getting past his arse no matter how hard you try.

Eventually players are able to find a message in a bottle indicating his daughter's whereabouts, which on the original Nintendo 64 version of the game then triggers an unskippable thirty-second cutscene entirely focused on the king making grunting noises ('Wubhu, Wubhu, Wubhu, Wubhu…') as he makes an effort to scooch his bottom maybe two feet to the side to let you pass. King Zora's arse is not only integral to the level design of *Ocarina of Time*, one of the most critically acclaimed games of all time, it's also the only arse in the series' history to get its own thirty-second-long cutscene.

HORIZON ZERO DAWN

▤ Aloy

In *Horizon Zero Dawn* you play Aloy, a woman born into a matriarchal society but living without a mother, which means she has spent much of her life as a social outcast before eventually setting out on a grand adventure to find out the origins of her world.

One has to imagine that her time as an outcast has given her a butt built to resist the elements. She's able to sit on hard surfaces, to resist the elements without shelter, and ride without a traditional saddle. You might think that she has a butt with some fat on it rather than pure toned muscle, but this doesn't match her build as we see it in-game, as well as the sheer level of physical ability she showcases during her adventure.

So, how do we reconcile a butt that's toned but also resistant to pain and the elements? Simple – her muscular butt is calloused and hardened by years of rough treatment. She's not been moisturising, she's not had comfy beds or chairs to sit on. This is a rock-solid butt, hard as stone, ready to take on any challenge the world might have for her.

RAYMAN

Rayman

When it comes to nineties' video-game protagonists, Rayman was probably one of the most universally enjoyed for a time. With his beautifully-animated platforming and pleasant demeanour, he was just an all-around nice character to play as.

One of the most obvious aspects of Rayman's design is his lack of arms, lack of legs, and, particularly, lack of butt. While there is no canon explanation for this within the lore of the games themselves, some interesting stories about scrapped concepts for Rayman shed some light on how our protagonist ended up missing many of the most important parts of the body.

If we dive back to a few years before the release of the original Rayman, creator Michel Ancel initially envisioned the narrative of the game as being about a young human boy called Jimmy who created the imaginatively titled online world

Hereitscool. The idea was that, when the world becomes infected with a computer virus, Jimmy would travel into the world of the computer and inhabit the body of Rayman, his in-game avatar.

Now, the developers may try and tell you Jimmy's lack of arms, legs and butt was due to a technical limitation on the hardware, but the reason actually may be to keep the most important parts of him grounded in the real world. He is physically sitting at his computer while on this in-game adventure, and by having a butt that's grounded, legs planted firm and arms resting on the desk, he won't lose sight of the fact this is not his reality.

They scrapped the Jimmy plot before *Rayman* was released, but its legacy lives on with Rayman's lack of a butt.

SCUM

Tena Žigmundovac
Marketing manager at Gamepires

When *SCUM* was released back in the summer of 2018, it first gained notoriety from a bug that plagued it for a short time. Player-characters start off completely naked and, due to the bug, each time a player logged on their character's penis would grow slightly larger. This story understandably caught attention, and is a big part of why many people know about the game.

Developed by Gamepires and Croteam, *SCUM* is an online multiplayer game where players try to survive as long as they can, collecting resources to protect themselves and fighting off anyone who gets too close to them.

Tena Žigmundovac, marketing manager at Gamepires, explained the development team's approach to butts in the game. She says when it came to adding uncensored butts to *SCUM*, it wasn't a case of any additional work. 'All the character models we made were nude anyway, so we didn't have to spend much time modelling the butts separately,' Tena reveals. 'We had to go out of our way to create a pooping animation, and we had to make the sounds that go with a game that implements realistic pooping, but that butt-specific work took us at most one afternoon. Our character model already had a butt, we just had to do a couple of things to make it functional in-game.'

One of the things that's interesting about *SCUM* is that the characters can all be played fully naked, and their butts are never pixelated, which

makes them a pretty unique case. Sure, you can turn on pixelation, but it's not a requirement. Many other games in this book, notably *Saints Row 4,* allow for nude characters but hide the butts away behind pixelation. So how hard was the decision to make all of *SCUM*'s butts so visible?

'It was a surprisingly easy choice. Our thinking was that we wanted our characters to have full body-realism. It's the reason we've paid so much attention to details like the digestive process, and it just made sense to extend that visibility and realism to the butt. A butt that is not visible is not realistic.'

SCUM doesn't do butts perfectly, however, with the unfortunate absence of realistic levels of jiggle on larger butts. According to Tena, it's mainly because calculating custom levels of jiggle based on butt size would have been a lot of extra work and risked causing the game to break.

'We have bounce physics on the stomachs, but unfortunately not the butts. We wanted to ensure that the game worked as realistically as possible, but because you can make your character as thin or fat as you want, changing the butt size, butt-bounce physics would just have been an additional complication to overcome.

'The type of butt depends on how fat or thin your character is, as well as if he has any muscle definition or not. Right now we're working hard on implementing female characters in the game as well, and their butts will work on the same principle.'

SCUM's butts are functional as well as aesthetic. While much of the world views defecation as taboo, SCUM's developers have not shied away from the topic. Had any players given a negative response to the accuracy of the nude-pooping in the game?

'Most people thought it was funny,' says Tena. 'We do have a full metabolism system in the game where your character has to not only eat but keep an eye on the kind and quality of food. You have to eat enough protein, you might stuff yourself with carbs if you're gonna run around a lot, and you have to be careful to stay hydrated. Fans acknowledge that pooping afterwards is a natural part of that realism.'

While the butt shadows in SCUM are fairly pronounced, they don't seem to change much in different situations. As seen in Tracer in Overwatch, dynamic butt shadows produce more variety, but they also require some oddly specific tricks to pull off correctly. I was unsurprised to learn that the butt shadows in SCUM are not dynamic – they're 'prebaked' shadows, which means the shadow is drawn onto the character model rather than being cast by the light source.

SCUM is available on Steam and is one of the few open-world games where you can stare freely at a gloriously uncensored butt.

BEYOND GOOD & EVIL

Jade

In the original *Beyond Good & Evil*, the playable protagonist Jade is a reporter who also helps her adoptive uncle, Pey'j, run an orphanage on a small, secluded island. Jade works as a photo-journalist, taking pictures of rare creatures and important events to get by, as well as running around looking after the needs of a very energetic group of children.

The fact that Jade works in two active roles is important, because her butt is probably the best of any freelance journalist in the world.

For most freelance journalists, the typical workday involves sitting on your arse all day writing, researching, filling out invoices and chugging coffee. Most would struggle to sprint from home to the shops, let alone do the hyper-flexible spin kicks Jade performs. Most journalists are still writing at 4 a.m., trying to find freelance gigs to fill out the month, too tired to get to the gym. However, Jade's lifestyle of running around alien government space-bases and chasing down misbehaving children has given her the firm, round buttocks most journalists spend more time reporting on than possessing themselves.

What? Most journalists don't report on butts? What disgraceful news!

Pey'j

As well as running a small community orphanage, human–pig hybrid Pey'j works as the head of a secret organisation trying to take down a corrupt, evil alien-controlled government. In his spare time, however, he is an inventor. It's the latter of these activities that is relevant to our butt discussion.

Fairly near the beginning of *Beyond Good & Evil*, Pey'j introduces us to his Jet-Boots, an invention which apparently represents the culmination of his life's inventions, and frankly they're both beautiful and amazing.

As you might have guessed, the Jet-Boots act as a form of propulsion, lifting the wearer off the ground, but the important thing to us is how they are powered. Pey'j creates a special pair of trousers to wear with them, with a section covering his butt that collects methane expulsions, stores them, then uses them as the fuel source for the Jet-Boots. Yes, this big, farty pig-man is such a genius that he realised he could turn his rampant, unchecked flatulence into a source of functional power.

Pey'j made fart-powered Jet-Boots, and that's worthy of recognition. He took a bodily function often assumed to be uncouth and improper and turned it into the next leap forwards for science. That's proper smart thinking about how to use the butt to its fullest potential.

THE WITCHER

🎮 Geralt of Rivia

There's no need to say anything about protagonist Geralt's butt except that, from a purely aesthetic perspective, it might be the finest video-game behind there is.

This muscular silver fox has an impeccably toned body, perfectly sculpted from tip to toe, and his butt is not only exquisite but also shown off in unconcealed glory five minutes into playing *The Witcher 3*. He gets out the bath, he's glistening with hot, steamy water, and it's just kind of... there.

Geralt's butt is compact, muscular and perky, but not so much that it's tough to get a solid grip on; it's a soft yet strong handful of chiselled perfection. It's cute, too, with a crack that's basically the butt equivalent of dimples. It's just a textbook specimen of a gorgeous butt. No story-justification needed – sometimes a butt just looks really gorgeous and we have to take a minute to enjoy that.

XENOBLADE CHRONICLES 2

Rex

Xenoblade Chronicles 2 is a game about our hero, Rex, who works as a salvager. He's particularly adept at donning a diver's suit, swimming below the world and finding valuable treasures on lost wrecks. The central event of the game involves Rex exploring a wreck and finding a legendary living swordswoman, who becomes soul-bonded to him and is the key to saving the world. The real subject is whether butts float or sink.

You see, Rex frequently has to go underwater or below the Cloud Sea into areas of increased density. If Rex is going to be a good salvager, he needs to be able to sink effectively, and as a lot of weight is carried on the buttocks – particularly given that the rest of his body is very lithe – he needs to have the correct type of butt.

In-game, his butt appears to be pretty small and lean, which is the ideal kind of butt for him to have. Fat is less dense than muscle, so the greater proportion of fat you have on your butt, the more likely it is in water to tend towards floating.

So, the results of this scientific investigation? Common sense prevails: Rex must have a small, muscular butt because otherwise his cheeks would try to float up and rest on the water's surface.

HALO

Master Chief

Protagonist Petty Officer John-117, better known in the Halo series as Master Chief, is a faceless hero by design. His face is always obscured by his green-and-yellow helmet, making his identity and appearance a complete mystery. But his story is not about the man behind the mask, it's about what he represents as a symbol of hope to the cosmos. Sure, 117 is a genetically engineered super-soldier, but really he could be anyone who has the bravery and courage to put everything on the line and try to save those in need.

You might be wondering what this has to do with Master Chief's backside. In fact, everything about John's arse is just as nondescript as his name and faceless appearance. His butt is average in every possible way, not drawing attention by being too large or too small, too muscular or too bulbous. It supports his frame adequately, but ultimately it's an everyman butt.

Master Chief's backside is nondescript by design, however. The intention behind giving Master Chief an arse that doesn't stand out in any way is clear: it makes it easier for the player to project themselves onto the character. Absolutely anyone can play a Halo game and imagine themselves in his armour and in his shoes, and feel that they, too, have the potential to save the world.

Cortana

In the Halo series, Cortana is an artificial intelligence construct, developed by the United Nations Space Command (UNSC) and designed to be a partner for protagonist Master Chief on many of his missions across the galaxy. Usually presented in-game as a holographic depiction of a mostly nude humanoid woman, Cortana's appearance, including that of her butt, tends to change noticeably from one game to the next, and the possible reasons for that change are what make her butt interesting.

Over the first four Halo games, Cortana gradually becomes more sexualised, with more exaggerated feminine physical features in each new game in the series. Her boobs get larger, her hips smaller and, of course, her butt gets bigger and plumper. She's a non-physical being, however, so a number of questions are raised by her gradual increase in traditional attractiveness.

Why, as a non-physical being, would her level of attractiveness be important? Is being more attractive her choice, or is it dictated by the UNSC or Master Chief? Does she have the choice to self-edit her image or is her appearance being edited by outside forces?

There are clues in the Halo games themselves as to who is in control of Cortana's appearance and how this is reflected in her butt. By the time we get to *Halo 3*, Cortana has been disconnected from her original network, suggesting that her image is now self-regulated rather than updated by outside forces. In *Halo 4*, the game's plot centres quite heavily around Cortana's growing relationship with Master Chief, due to the amount of time she spends living in his head, and by the end of the game she has moulded her image to his tastes in women, with his ideal female butt. However, her appearance changes again in *Halo 5*, where she eventually rebels against Master Chief, pushing for different ideals to his, and moves away from her peak sexualisation to a more muscular build, presenting herself as a powerful and stable woman, one not to be messed with, with a butt that can support her new strong and defiant form.

THOMAS WAS ALONE

Mike Bithell

Back in the summer of 2012, indie developer Mike Bithell released his first commercially and critically successful game, *Thomas Was Alone*. The game features a series of colourful rectangles exploring various platforming environments against a spoken narrative that tells the story and gives the rectangles distinct personalities.

While the rectangles are pretty plain in design, and don't show anything that the average player would likely recognise as a butt, Mike explains with feeling how even a colourful rectangle can be rich ground for analysis of the butt-design process.

Several years ago I made a game called *Thomas Was Alone.* It was about rectangles, and feelings, and stuff like that.

Let's start with Thomas, a small, red rectangle who is slightly taller than he is wide. I think the thing with Thomas that defines him is his optimism, so his is an uplifting butt. It's a butt that has hopes and dreams, and a general interest in what's in front of him. It's not the greatest butt in the world, it doesn't help him jump highest or fit into the smallest spaces. It's just a general, all-purpose, average butt.

That kind of butt doesn't necessarily get the kind of praise it deserves, and that's something I feel very strongly about when designing video games – that we need to celebrate these kinds of butts. We need to celebrate these more normal, more human butts, and that's why I went with that for Thomas, my title character.

So, when I design a character, I design them from the butt outwards. The butt is the root from which everything else grows. For the first character, I knew we needed to start with an everyman butt, a butt everyone could relate to, a butt that could support the story.

The first prototype for *Thomas Was Alone* went up online as a Flash game, and people were already talking about what the characters were like and inventing little stories. Assuming that, for example, one character was short and had a Napoleon complex was stuff that we never intentionally put in the game, but people interpret – you know. And when people see a rectangle and interpret it as a person, people are then going to assume that humanoid rectangle has a butt.

For me, directly revealing the butts – if we were to show them rather than abstract them as rectangles – would compromise my artistic vision. I think it has to be a butt that exists as a sort of Schrödinger's butt, a butt that could either be there or not be there – the act of not knowing is what makes it interesting. This is why I never show the butts, but keep them in mind when designing my characters. For me, having the character be just a plain rectangle is not so much an absence of butt, but a lack of visible presence of butt.

Next let's talk about Chris, a small, orange, square character. Chris has a stick up his butt. He's grumpy, he's unhappy about his station in life, he's a bit smaller and a bit more rubbish than Thomas, and he's not confident. For me, that means Chris is someone with a subpar butt, both in terms of distance from the ground (because he's shorter) and sheer quality. He's never relaxed, and that tension results in an eternally tensed and clenched butt. I think the way you'd ultimately know if you'd made a meaningful connection with Chris is if he unclenches his butt around you, if he ever truly relaxes.

Thomas is always moving in front of Chris, so he's being shown that butt a lot, so he's following it in both a physical and emotional sense, which is part of his anger. If you have to traverse the world following and jumping on people, Chris is going to very literally be in the shadow of Thomas's butt. That struggle, of Chris living in Thomas's butt shadow, is crucial to understanding the game in its first twenty to thirty levels.

I think Thomas is oblivious to this whole Chris–butt struggle. I'm a big believer that the artist should never try and say what the correct interpretation of the art is, but at least in my thinking, when designing the game, Thomas is ignorant of the situation. His mind is on other things, his butt is not a factor in his thinking in his own life, it's not important to him the same way it is to Chris, hence him not realising Chris might be having this struggle.

The next butt is that of John, a tall, thin yellow rectangle. We're now talking about a more athletic butt, the strongest butt in the game from a muscular perspective. John can jump high, and he's proud of it, and proud of his butt.

He's sort of part way between a high jumper and a sprinter, where it's not necessarily about volume of butt muscle, but its quality. John has optimised what nature has given him.

To be born with a great butt is impressive, but it's those who create their own great butt that are truly awesome.

John's character is very aware of his butt and of his physical superiority, he's the first character we meet who takes pride in his butt. It's that pride in his butt that defines him.

Next we have Claire, a large, blue square whose butt is pretty important and unique compared to others in the game. I'm aware that a lot of people view Claire as a larger lady, with a larger backside, but that wasn't something I initially intended, nor are the lines of dialogue people think imply that about her.

Claire was not designed story wise to have her shape, but was designed, from a gameplay perspective, to be able to float on water and have other characters float on top of her. For that, she needed to be scaled up. That said, I am totally fine with that interpretation of Claire as a larger lady, and it does make sense; this is a buoyant butt we're talking about, and fatty tissue in large amounts is more buoyant than muscle.

Claire is very self-confident. She views herself as a superhero and believes she can rescue everyone, and that confidence applies to her butt, too. What's interesting is that she ultimately realises how much of an asset that arse is. She realises it makes her powerful, gives her strength and makes her useful. She has a super-powered butt, and super-powered butts are one of video games' remaining undiscovered mechanics.

The thing about the lack of butt-tech in games is that the development technology really has had to catch up. You just couldn't have done Claire's butt justice on any of the past generations of gaming hardware. It's really only now, thanks to the modern pile of consoles, that you can deliver the true butt experience. I think the Nintendo 64 could have achieved a surface-level butt, but if you're going to dive deep into what butts can and should be, then you need a much more powerful system. The butt subtext alone is just such a resource drain. You really need the subtext engine to make butts work properly, and that's why no true art game about butts was made before 2012.

You have to push and push, and really get it out, that butt tech. You put in the effort, you strain, and that's what *Thomas Was Alone* is – it's the result of that pushing and straining hard.

Sometimes you make a game and it comes out too easy, and it's just wet, uninspired and it's weak as a result. While in the moment that's easier, you don't get the same level of satisfaction as if you produce something really solid. You want something that really holds together, that is compact and perfect.

Next up, a particular fan-favourite butt has been Laura's, particularly in relation to Chris's butt. These two characters fall in love, and it's interesting viewing that through the lens of their butts.

There are two schools of thought regarding Laura – whether she is very short and wide, or tall, thin and lying down. You can't jump while lying down, so I don't view her lying down. This game is about realism, about real-world physics, and frankly I'm embarrassed by anyone who sees her that way in my very realistic video game.

So to me she's a very wide character. I think of Laura's butt more as a concept, and not as a physical form. A concept of a butt. She's short and wide, but her butt is more of a concept than something directly presented by her shape. Her butt is bouncy though.

The final butt is Sarah's, and she's somewhat of an elephant in the room. She's a double-jumper, and it's never explained in the canon of the game how she double-jumps. Obviously, however, that would require a great degree of butt control.

I don't want to agree or disagree with the theory that her double-jump is caused by flatulence, a second burst of propulsion in mid-air, because for me that's a mystery which should be left up to fan interpretation. As a designer, it wasn't directly flatulence so much, simply because I am an artist and fart jokes are just far too easy. I didn't want to go the easy route. Even if her double-jumping was a fart joke, I would right now be pretending the reason was something much more clever and hipster-sounding.

For me, the source of the double-jump is the butt; as mentioned, all my characters start with the butt and works outwards. This is more about anticipation and intent, the idea that we can know what a character is thinking, planning and feeling through their butt. There are some great resources out there about this – *The Animator's Survival Kit* has a whole chapter dedicated to butt intent. Now with Sarah, her butt's intention is simply to be higher up. So through the power of will and of butts, she literally ascends.

I'm a spiritual man, and I believe that where there's a butt, there's a way. If you set your butt to a task, and you don't stop, there is nothing your butt can't achieve. For me, that's what the entire character is about. Through sheer force of will, she's double-jumping through the air. The mechanics of that are irrelevant – maybe it is flatulence, I'll leave the question of mechanics up to the players.

Talking more broadly about the game as a whole with regard to butts, at its core this game is in part a story of a group of people coming together and learning that every butt is valid, important, and useful. That's kind of a shallow reading, but it's definitely there. For me, butts are a unifying force, and that is present in the text of the story. I call it a shallow reading because I think it misses that in searching for a defining moral of the story, you miss the fact that the true butt of the game is right there in your face, and you can't even see it.

What I actually did when creating *Thomas Was Alone* was create the game using the Hindenburg Butt Model, which is a traditional storytelling device most people aren't aware of. What it essentially defines is the way a story is told, within the curve of the emotional reaction to a butt. However, it also follows the shape of a butt, when plotted out onto a graph. It's a fractal butt; it's butts all the way down.

Imagine a graph, if you will, where the Y-axis is emotional intensity and storytelling, and the X-axis is time. When we play *Thomas Was Alone*, we very carefully make our story arc map out on the graph as a pair of buttocks. You start very intense, then we drop that down, we introduce boring elements of gameplay in order to lower the level of interest in the story. Then about half way through the game we rise back up again into a peak, though it's not as high, not as intense, as the original start-point of the adventure. It's a very quick, sharp rise to this interesting point, then intentionally a quick, sharp drop back down to boring gameplay. We poke at that crevice of emotional intensity incredibly briefly, then return back down. Just a taste of that crevice. Towards the end of the game we raise that emotional intensity back up to where it began, so you leave the game feeling as emotionally interested as when you started, which is really all we can hope for.

That is the Hindenburg Butt Model. It's how we tell stories, and I would recommend people google it for further research.

DEAD SPACE

Puker

Dead Space 2's adversaries, the Pukers, are fascinating in terms of butt designs because, while they have a standard set of human buttocks, these are not symmetrically placed on the body.

The Puker is a humanoid creature with a partially decomposed front exposing some of its inner organs. When we look down to the waist, it still has both human legs but it has grown a new, tendril-like third leg out of its intestines and other gross, slimy, meat materials.

It prioritises walking on one human leg and the tendril leg, leaving the other human leg as more of a support and shifting the buttocks towards one side of the body rather than a central position. The two active legs and the buttocks are also partially fused shut, reducing the ability to move in a normal human fashion.

What is particularly interesting about this butt design is what it implies about the function-over-form nature of *Dead Space*'s enemies. The fused legs and butt gives the Puker what is ultimately a larger and sturdier set of legs, which tells us that short-term function is the driving force of this creature's design.

The asymmetrical position of the Puker's butt shows the player that the Puker isn't focused on improving its existing human form, but is in fact willing to discard the human elements entirely for its own view of the perfect creature. But the asymmetrical butt also represents the instability of the creature. Sure, the Puker can do massive damage, but it lacks a human core that would give it stability, so it's also very fragile. In the pursuit of power, it has lost the very thing that kept it human and strongly grounded.

ANIMAL CROSSING

⊞ Isabelle

In Isabelle's original incarnation, there is no way her butt would have made the list of gaming rear ends. However, the fact that Isabelle, the *Animal Crossing* mayor's assistant, was made into a fighter in *Super Smash Bros. Ultimate* considerably changed things. Isabelle has now had two careers, and they have brought conflicting butt requirements with them. She has two jobs, and they need two different butts.

In *Animal Crossing*, Isabelle is shown to be a secretary and assistant who runs things very much by the books. She's in fairly good physical health, likely a result of running around town attending to citizens' needs and managing events for the game's players, but her outfit and pencil-straight figure give no real information on her buttocks, so we have to look to more abstract clues for this information.

Isabelle is a workaholic, which means she has to spend a lot of time sitting down handling paperwork. For that to be as comfortable as possible, her butt has to be more focused on fat rather than muscle, simply so it has some additional cushioning. We know her butt isn't large enough to leave an impression on her pencil skirt, so we can assume it's neither super-large nor super-muscular.

However, with her introduction to Smash Bros., things have to change slightly. She's now a competitive fighter, and surely that requires butt muscles to power her attacks? Actually, no. As it turns out, that same small butt does just fine. If you look at Isabelle's move-set in *Smash*, her moves are all based around items used to great effect. You don't need a muscular butt to throw a bucket of water, set off a party popper, throw out a fishing line or construct a stop sign

So while many will have assumed that Isabelle would need a big-muscle butt to be a fighter, it turns out she can keep her small, comfortable behind for secretarial duties yet still stand toe-to-toe with her enemy combatants. It's a no-compromise butt.

Tom Nook

If you've ever played an Animal Crossing game, you'll know very well who Tom Nook is. A real estate agent and debt collector, the unscrupulous raccoon finds people who are new to town and gets them a house; then, whether they ask for it or not, he renovates the house and expects the owners to work off their debt in his service, at least prior to *AC: New Horizons*, where he waits for players to ask for new upgrades. He's the taskmaster driving forward your time in Animal Crossing's otherwise unfriendly world. While Tom Nook's butt is rarely ever seen in official artwork, a lot of three-quarters-perspective front-facing artwork shows he has quite a pronounced belly. This isn't a problem – be happy no matter your size – but it does tell us that he probably has a pretty chunky bottom, too, and it's not hard to imagine why that might be. Tom Nook gets rich off those in need, so it stands to reason he would be a man of wealth and excess. Even in *New Horizons*, where he makes a big deal of not charging you interest or forcing upgrades on you, he never lifts a finger around the island like the other residents, making a living off your hard work.

DARK SOULS

Chosen Undead

In the original *Dark Souls*, you play as the Chosen Undead, a presumed descendant of one of the original lords – four ancient beings – who claimed the Dark Soul, which gave its wielder a huge amount of power. The subject of a prophecy, the Chosen Undead is expected to undertake a pilgrimage to ring The Bell of Awakening, although they don't initially know why.

When it comes to reviewing the butt of the Chosen Undead, we have to answer a fundamental question about the character: which is a truer version of the character – their Hollow or human form?

In *Dark Souls*, you start the game undead, a reanimated corpse shrivelled-up like a raisin; a wrinkly, skinny zombie with barely any meat on its bones. However, by using humanity, the player can temporarily bring back their appearance to that of a regular human, until that humanity is once again lost.

While the human form butt of the Chosen Undead has by far the nicer butt, with tone, bounce, shape and a firm handful to hold, the true butt of the character is that of their undead form. It's how you start the game, and it's the default state you seem to always revert to. Without using humanity from your inventory, you'll always end up undead; becoming human only happens with outside intervention.

With all this in mind, there's no choice but to dismiss the pretty decent human butt of the Chosen Undead and instead give this game's main butt a low rating.

Sorry, I'm just not into wrinkly, skinny, hollow zombie butts.

Chaos Witch Quelaag

In the original *Dark Souls*, Chaos Witch Quelaag is a spider-woman boss found down in Blighttown, an area down in the depths of the game's map and full of horrible, murky poisons. A daughter of the Witch of Izalith, she was transformed into her monstrous form by the flames of chaos.

This spider–human hybrid, who fights you only to protect her comatose sister, has by far my favourite butt in all of *Dark Souls,* because it is absolutely HUGE. Okay, so her giant butt is actually a giant spider, but it's still her butt and it's still huge. It starts right at the base of her back, where the human back would normally flare out towards the hips and mark the beginning of the buttocks, and is the connecting point between her human torso and her many, many spider legs.

Quelaag's butt is perhaps twenty or thirty times the size of her human body, making it a serious contender for biggest butt in gaming. Also, it's on fire.

I do love a huge, smoking, hot butt.

BLOODBORNE

Guest Butt Critic
Jim Sterling

YouTuber and video-game reviewer Jim Sterling has had a long and varied career in the video-game industry. Previously working at websites such as Destructoid, over the past few years Jim has made a name for himself as a solo content creator, focusing largely on video and podcast production.

Jim Sterling's best-known piece of content is a weekly video series called *The Jimquisition*, where he dresses up in a suit and sings his own praises while critiquing aspects of the video-game industry; he also does video impressions of games and is one of the hosts of the crude video-game news podcast *Podquisition*.

Maneater Boar

When it comes to arses, FromSoftware has always been on point. From the weaponised posterior of the Asylum Demon to the softly folded crevices of *Dark Souls 2*'s cycloptic ogres, titanic tushies have practically been the *Souls* series' stock and trade. When it comes to kingly keisters, however, none can surpass that of the humble pig... which is a lot less humble and a lot more horrifying in the *Souls* world.

In *Dark Souls*, we're introduced to the Armored Tusk, an oversized porcine peril that, true to its name, bears a vicious set of tusks and is covered almost completely in armour. The keyword is 'almost', for its ripe rump is left unprotected and waiting for the scythes, blades, clubs and eager fists of many an undead adventurer. At least, this is true of the first Armored Tusks; the other two encountered in the game are more shy about exposing their bitter ends, covering up their tender portions with a bit more armour, which they presumably found lying around.

For a full-on booty bonanza, however, you want to travel to the eldritch land of Yharnam, where Goliath Pigs and Maneater Boars roam. *Bloodborne*'s piggy pursuers are an altogether less clothed affair, and their hindquarters have been rendered in juicy detail. The real derrière delights are found in *Bloodborne*'s visceral attack system. Charging up an attack on the pig's vulnerable hindquarters will see the player-character's arm transform into a beastly, clawed appendage that is thrust entirely inside the tender tunnels. Seriously, they go right up it. RIGHT UP IT! The pigs of *Bloodborne* do not just have exquisitely rendered, suitably disgusting butts, their gasping gapers are a key tactical feature. If you ever wanted to be elbow-deep in a car-sized pig, *Bloodborne* is the game for you!

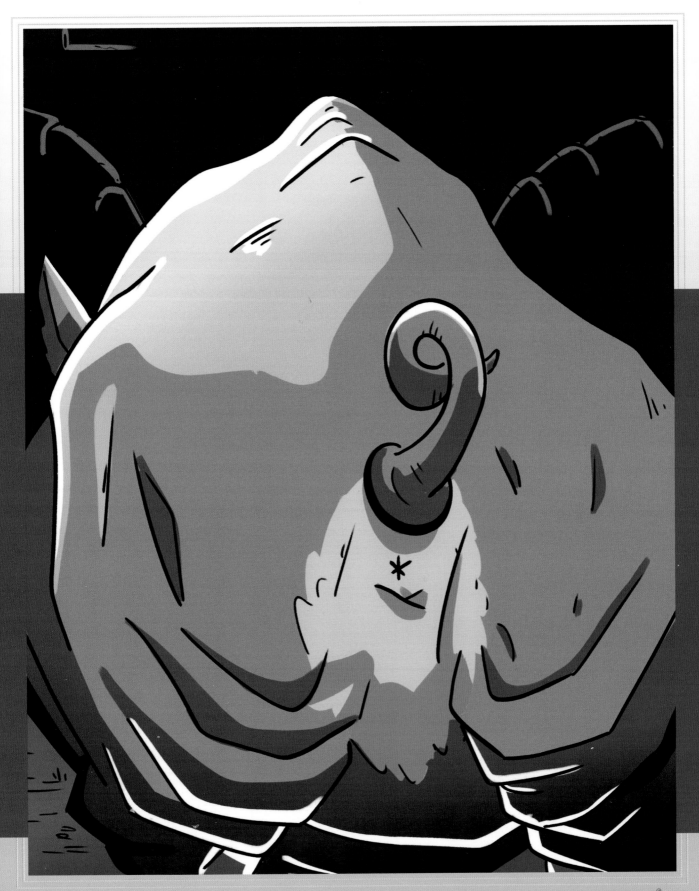

Guest Butt Critic
Brian Altano

Brian Altano is best known for his work reviewing and discussing video games for IGN, one of the world's biggest gaming outlets. He's also a musician and features on numerous popular podcasts including *The Comedy Button* and *Weird Heat*. He has now written a beautiful poem for this book about *Bloodborne*, a difficult and challenging action-platformer, set in a world where horrific eldritch abominations roam the street, eliciting the physical response to fear that Brian has contemplated in this work.

A Bloodborne Hunter's Pledge
(To Not Shit His Pants from Fear)

The moon ascends, its heart is black,

A Hunter darts between the cracks,

His shrivelled buttocks on his back.

He promises to keep this pact:

A Hunter shall not shat his rump!

Past crumbled ruins and tortured stumps,

Through creaking trees and dreams that thump,

A Hunter mustn't shat his rump!

A Hunter shall not soil his slacks!

Near mangled mares with hooves that clack

When pressing forth or doubling back,

This Hunter shall not soil his slacks!

A Hunter shall not stool his seat!

Contorted beasts with gnashing teeth

Nor shrieking witches' poison teats

Can make this Hunter stool his seat!

A Hunter shall not dook his bottom!

Though snakes and rats and spiders seek him

While Yharnam screams from spring to autumn,

A Hunter never dooks his bottom!

A Hunter shall not brick his trousers!

When wretched men traverse these towers

With pitchforks, torches lit, they scour,

This Hunter wouldn't brick his trousers!

A Hunter shall not deuce his knickers!

Past Ludwig, Rom, Kos, Paarl and Vicar,

For when the souls of Hemwick flicker

A Hunter will not deuce his knickers!

But sometimes fear and stress collide

To manifest an arse surprise,

And suddenly, a poop resides.

Farewell, good Hunter's pants – you died.

🎮 Bloodborne Disc Butt

If you own a physical copy of *Bloodborne*, rather than a digital one, you might want to give it a slightly closer look, as it's hiding a butt-based secret.

Sure, there's a picture on the disc of the main character posing with a big slicing blade, but what's more important is what's missing from the picture: the protagonist has no bottom, and there's a hole where his buttocks would be.

While this alone may not seem like much, place a pair of fingers behind the hole and before you know it there's a butt on this vicious monster assassin, and a fully exposed butt with no clothing at that. What a rare treat in video games.

The joy of this hidden butt is that, because you fill in the gap, you can dictate what kind of butt it is. Does the butt push through the gap because it's so large? What skin colour is the butt? You get to decide, because the *Bloodborne* game disc is a choose-your-own butt adventure.

F-ZERO

Captain Falcon

Somewhat of an unofficial mascot for the F-Zero series, Captain Falcon's butt got its start in futuristic racing machines, but really got to shine in the Super Smash Bros. fighting game series.

Captain Falcon is one of those incredibly rare fighting-game characters whose butt actually works perfectly with the rest of his exaggeratedly muscular body. The Captain has the muscular equivalent of an hourglass figure, with his large abs and buttocks defining a small and lean core, and his pecs and legs flaring outwards as wider muscle groups that transfer power very efficiently between his legs and arms to deliver incredibly powerful attacks.

If you watch Captain Falcon execute a 'Falcon Punch', the whole attack begins in the legs with a powerful stance and low centre of gravity. He shifts his weight to one side, then uses his legs to shift it in the direction of his punch. This is where his butt and glutes come in, tensing up to ensure none of that power is lost and allowing him to use his arms and legs in harmony to deliver a more powerful smash attack than perhaps any other character in Smash Bros. That said, with a butt that lean, let's hope the driver's seat in the Blue Falcon has good padding, because the Captain sure hasn't got much padding of his own.

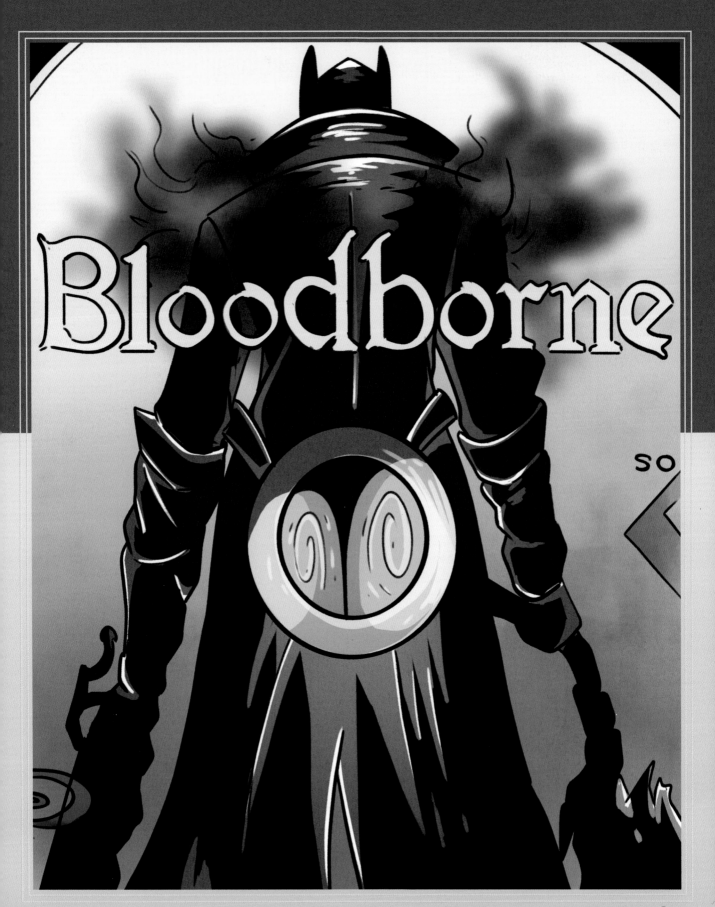

SO

THINGS I LEARNED FROM MARIO'S BUTT

POKÉMON

Spoink

The tale of the Pokémon character Spoink is a rather sad one, and is often overlooked due to the distraction of the creature's endearing visual design. A small, grey pig-blob with arms and an orb on his head, Spoink is an absolutely adorable Pokémon to look at. From its sweet, innocent face to the way it blushes, this Pokémon looks as cute as a button.

However, if you look further down its design, you'll see its butt is, by contrast, quite sad. From the waist down, Spoink's body is just a single spring. This acts as both the legs and the butt of the creature, forming not only the core of its body but also the limb with which it gets around. There are dark undertones to this cute-looking spring: according to the Pokédex, Spoink must never stop bouncing on that butt-tail or it will die.

Yes, you heard me right: if this cute children's creature ever stops bouncing, day or night, even once, it's instant death.

This is because it's the springing motion that powers the pumping of Spoink's heart, with each bounce keeping the creature alive for just one moment longer. This makes Spoink's butt the most important part of its body; this is a butt that not only never quits, but literally *cannot* ever quit, for fear of terminal heart failure.

Koffing

The original-generation Pokémon Koffing makes for an odd butt discussion because you could argue that it has many very visible butts, none more or less valid than the others.

One thing we know for sure about Koffing is that it has a mouth, right there on the front next to its eyes, and the fact it can eat 'berries' and 'candy' in the Pokémon games tells us this is a functional mouth and must lead to some sort of digestive system. If Koffing can eat, it has to have a butt of some kind, and the answer to where that butt is should be easy. Every one of those knobbly, noxious, gas-expelling bumps on its body is a butt.

Think about it, if you've ever emitted a noxious gas, chances are high it came from your bottom. The reason Koffing is such an effective Pokémon is because it has such dexterous control of its foul, gas-spewing abilities. Koffing is only as strong a Pokémon as it is because, basically, it can fart in any direction at will.

▨ Ditto

If you've ever played one of the Pokémon games, there's a good chance you're aware of Ditto, the pink-blob Pokémon that has a single but powerful trick up its sleeve: transformation. It likes to transform into other Pokémon, gaining their abilities and attacks until changing back to its original form at the end of the fight.

The fact that when Ditto transforms it is able to use the target Pokémon's moves, and be mating partners with any species in the mainline Pokémon games, suggests something interesting: Ditto isn't just changing its appearance, it is actively changing its entire physiology to match its target.

Unlike Mass Effect's Liara, who we butt-reviewed earlier in this book, this butt is a real, tangible butt, post-transformation. We noted (on p. 38) that Liara's butt looks like different butts due to mind-manipulation, but Ditto is the real deal. Not only can Ditto appear to have the arse of any Pokémon, it can have that butt's functionality too.

Ditto truly is the beast of infinite butts, for he can inhabit any butt in the universe. That's a terrifyingly strong power to possess.

PATRICK

The Proctology Training Robot, University of Florida

A lot of video-game butts are silly and amusing, but ultimately not changing the world. Patrick, the proctology training robot, is a little different.

Built by the University of Florida, Patrick is a physical prop, an anatomically correct training model, housing buttons and pressure sensors, of a male backside. The robot is placed against a screen running a video game showing the upper torso of Patrick. When Patrick's butt gets injured, the model butt reacts in real time as the trainee doctors practice how to fix a damaged arse.

Doctors can perform rectal exams on Patrick, receiving real-time feedback on their medical performance and ratings on how well they treat and diagnose their patient.

Patrick is helping doctors get better at poking around up there before helping real world patients, and that feels like world-changing research. It's reassuring to know that doctors have Patrick to practise on rather than having to make their first experiments on real people.

SPIDER-MAN PS4

Spider-Man

A huge part of many superheroes' character arcs is keeping their true identity a secret. By hiding behind a mask, heroes like Spider-Man can do what they feel is right, saving the people of the world, without drawing the attention of those who would stand in the way of their mission. This is no different for Peter Parker, AKA Spider-Man.

So, let's talk about Spider-Man's butt. It's undeniable that the vast majority of Spidey's Lycra super-suits are pretty form-fitting, at times ludicrously so. He falls into the group of characters who, for their Lycra suit to make sense, would probably have had to glue their suits to the inside of their butt cheeks just to get that glorious level of suit-emphasis definition.

But strip away the suit Spidey has glued into his butt and Peter Parker actually has a kind of forgettable arse. That's not to say it doesn't look really nice – his arse is toned and has some muscle – but not in any way that really stands out from any other nice arse that anyone could pick from a line-up.

This is important, because if Spider-Man had such an amazingly perfect butt that it was identifiable by the general public, the chances of Peter keeping himself secret without wearing puffy trousers every day would be far slimmer.

So an average, nice butt for a superhero is a blessing, not a curse. You can have a good butt, but you can't have a memorably perfect arse.

Mister Negative

In Marvel's Spider-Man on PS4, our primary game-long antagonist is Mister Negative, the evil alter ego of philanthropist Martin Li. While we never get a great look at Mister Negative's butt, we do get a couple of moments to look at Li's backside. Li himself has a comfortably average butt – on the lean side, reasonably toned, relatively flat but with decent cheek definition regardless.

With the above in mind, we know Mister Negative is the inverse of Li in colour, personality – and, one assumes, butt. If we invert all the features

of Martin Li's butt, we are lead to believe Mister Negative has a butt on the larger side of average, protruding, with minimal cheek definition. His butt is basically one big protruding butt cheek with just a tiny, mini crease in the centre.

From this, it's easier to understand why he's so angry when he's Mister Negative. You'd be furious, too, if a science experiment gone wrong meant you had basically one subpar butt cheek for the rest of your days.

WII

Mii

Nintendo's Mii characters are simple avatars that players can customise to look like themselves – the perfect storm of simplicity and projection. Introduced with the Wii, these cartoon characters, and their ability to play in launch title *Wii Sports*, are a great, non-threatening way to get non-gamers excited about playing video games. That non-threatening attitude extends towards their butt – or, rather, lack of butt.

As standard, a Mii doesn't actually have a butt. This is surely deliberate. By having a universal lack of butt, any player can project on to their Mii. While a butt-design slider would have been preferable to no butt, it's important to remember

that these characters are on a family console. While in private it would be fun to crank up a butt-size slider on my Mii to eleven, custom butt-sizes might lead to awkward conversations over family dinner.

As Miis don't really have a butt of their own, I decided to investigate whether it was possible to give them a bespoke butt. First I tried to use face pieces to create a butt-shape I could place on the butt region, but Miis don't support moving facial features that low down on the figure. Still, you can give your Mii a surprisingly accurate butt on their face, with a variety of possible styles, so I suppose you could still give your Mii the perfect butt – just not on the part of the body you might have wanted it.

🎮 Wii Fit Trainer

When *Wii Fit* was first released, it was undeniably a cultural touchstone. For households who had already bought a Wii for *Wii Sports*, *Wii Fit* offered an at-home framework for exercise and health tracking that managed to gamify healthy living in a way that captured minds and brought in tens of millions of sales.

There's something non-threatening about the butts in *Wii Fit*, designed not to scare off people who may only be buying their second ever video game. Players are given a choice of a masculine or feminine character who acts as a personal trainer, leading you through yoga poses and updating you on your progress. So, let's talk about the importance of getting the design of a virtual personal trainer's butt just right. First, their body has to fit into a very particular body-design window; specifically, they have to be aspirational but not daunting. A big part of why *Wii Fit* works so well as a self-improvement tool is that, whether you choose the male trainer or the female one, you'll find their butts meet this requirement. They're impressive enough butts that the average person can look at them and say, *Yeah, I'd love it if my butt looked a little more like that*, without being so perfect that achieving such a butt feels so impossible it's not even worth trying for.

When we look at the female Wii Fit Trainer, her butt is curvaceous but not muscular. Her butt is small enough that her curves are considered traditionally flattering, but large enough that it doesn't send a message that you have to burn every inch of fat to have the butt of your dreams. Her butt has enough cushion to be comfortable, but enough shape to be aspirational. It's an achievable-aspirational butt.

The male Wii Fit Trainer has a smaller and squarer butt, less rounded but still not impossibly toned. He's not got the equivalent of butt-based abs, he's no Solid Snake in terms of rock-solid butt design, but his butt has minimal flab and a nice general shape. He's not stressed about building muscle but has burned off a little excess fat so his trousers can fit more comfortably. Again, an arse to aspire to, but not one that seems out of reach to most players.

Wii Fit succeeded as a gamified exercise tool because, when it comes to butts, it strikes just the right balance between aspiration and intimidation in the field of fitness.

Guest Butt Critic
Tim Gettys

Tim Gettys is co-founder of Kinda Funny Games, a video and podcast network he heads up alongside former IGN editor Greg Miller. A 2019 Forbes 30 Under 30 winner, Gettys spends his days sharing his opinions on video games with an enthusiastic audience. As a long-time fan of PlayStation exclusive games, Gettys couldn't resist writing about one of Sony's first exclusive characters, and exclusive butts.

THE CRASH BANDICOOT SERIES

Crash Bandicoot

Crash Bandicoot gets a bad rap. As an icon of nineties gaming, he is often mistakenly attributed a too-cool-for-school attitude that is actually a more appropriate assessment of Sonic the Hedgehog. Aside from his iconic megaphone commercials and crotch-chop idle-animation, Crash has always been more Looney Tunes than D-Generation X.

He is such a lovable, doofy idiot – from his oversized sneakers all the way up to that unkempt, spiky puff of hair. But somewhere in the middle is where fashion meets function. Let's talk about those jorts, baby!

For years we were limited to Mario running from left to right, with no real concept of what was going on with that plumber's crack. Then Crash comes along spending most of his time running away from the camera, giving us ample opportunity to appreciate video-game butts with some perspective. Over the course of the adventure, the bond strengthens between you, Crash and that sweet orange peach he is hiding in those jeans shorts. As you overcome obstacle after obstacle on your journey to... honestly, I don't really remember exactly what dumb plot device set the whole thing in motion, but I am sure it doesn't matter. What does matter is the dozen hours of gameplay you spend watching Crash's backside do what it does best – jumping, spinning and slamming into crates.

Crash Bandicoot was the first third-person game I ever played, and it introduced me to a whole new dimension of gaming. I have many fond memories of those bright-blue jorts and will forever appreciate the junk that is inside them.

THINGS I LEARNED FROM MARIO'S BUTT

UNCHARTED

🎮 Nathan Drake

Ohhh, Nathan Drake's arse – now that's some uncharted territory worth exploring.

Nathan Drake, the protagonist of the Uncharted games, has spent his life as a treasure hunter, exploring uncharted tombs and islands, so for him the idea of being the best adventurer out there was always a forgone conclusion.

Nathan Drake was actually born Nathan Morgan, but from a young age he and his brother became convinced they were descendants of famed treasure hunter Sir Francis Drake, and this driving belief has been the basis for much of Nathan's character. Of course, his determination to be unambiguously the best treasure hunter there is takes effort, dedication and, above all else, fitness. So it's no surprise that Nathan has an amazing butt, because he needs one to live up to his namesake.

Once you take on the surname of one of your idols, you don't really have a choice but to get working hard on living up to it. Once Nathan Morgan became Nathan Drake, he needed an arse that Sir Francis Drake would be proud of.

TOMB RAIDER

Lara Croft

One of gaming's first scantily clad protagonists, Lara Croft and her butt have undergone numerous reimaginings and redesigns over the years, with the changes in her butt design often lining up with the way her personality as a protagonist has shifted.

Looking back at the earliest examples of Lara Croft, her butt was simply a pointy triangle, not fit for sitting on or for touching. This is because in her earliest games Lara had no time for anything but action. No time for butt-touching companions, no sitting down to rest, just a big, pointy, unfunctional triangle.

Moving on to the *Tomb Raider: Anniversary* era, Lara has a much more rounded and softer butt, signifying the game's shift to more story-driven adventures, trying to make Lara more of a sympathetic protagonist with more complex motivations.

Finally, when we switch to the most recent incarnation of Lara Croft, she's wearing full-length trousers as a default look. This shows players that this version of the character is much less interested in having sex appeal and much more in being pragmatic and actually being good at raiding tombs. Her butt is no longer the star of the show, but we know from past games it's in there, somewhere. Today's Lara knows her butt can get the job done, and sees no need to show it off to prove it.

RED DEAD REDEMPTION

▣ John Marston

John Marston, protagonist of *Red Dead Redemption*, is a fairly handsome man. He's a rugged, Wild West outlaw and gunslinger with the sort of masculine face that's hard to resist. However, what's likely not to be terribly attractive is much of his skin, including that on his butt.

Before industrialisation had really kicked in, much of the Wild West subsisted on fairly limited diets. You might get some occasional veg and fruit, but a lot of the time people were surviving primarily on meat. Access to citrus fruit, in particular, was at times scarce, leading to frequent bouts of scurvy, a severe lack of vitamin C. Scurvy can cause symptoms including easy bruising, excess bleeding, discoloured skin patches and painful sores. Considering the rough-and-tumble nature of the Wild West, activities like sitting on hard ground, horse riding and tumbles in shoot-outs mean that John Marston's butt would be at an elevated risk of all of the above. While we never see Marston's butt uncovered, it's likely at least a little bruised and scabby. Maybe it's better to just keep to looking at his handsome face instead.

CONKER'S BAD FUR DAY

The Great Mighty Poo

The Great Mighty Poo is a boss enemy in the Nintendo 64 game *Conker's Bad Fur Day*, and he's exactly what he sounds like: a sentient lump of faecal matter.

Conker's Bad Fur Day was a Rare N64 game (both by nature of its highly adult content and the game's developer) about a foul-mouthed squirrel who ran around trying to find big, fat stacks of cash. Some way into the game he comes across The Great Mighty Poo, a sweetcorn-filled excrement monster who sings quite frankly amazing operatic tracks about bodily waste.

Now, our discussion of The Great Mighty Poo has less to do with discussing the character's own butt and more about the role that butts play in his story. The Great Mighty Poo simply could not exist without butts – that's a fact we can all agree on. He's clearly aware of the existence of butts, based on comments made during his songs, and he may well be the world's only truly butt-centric boss-fight. Sure, you might have to occasionally fight bosses where you attack their butts, but never before or since has a boss-fight entirely revolved around a butt and nothing else.

The Great Mighty Poo, an evil, villainous turd urgently in need of flushing, reminds us of the darker side of the booty. Everybody poops, and sometimes that poop is so evil it becomes a sentient poop-monster.

🎮 Berri

When you think of *Conker's Bad Fur Day* for the Nintendo 64, you tend to think of some of the standout moments. The *Saving Private Ryan* beach-sequence parody. The dulcet tones of the *Great Mighty Poo*. Conker attempting to jump onto a sunflower's heaving bosoms.

Yes, *Conker's Bad Fur Day* is chock-full of movie spoofs, musical numbers and bawdy humour – rather as if someone accidentally combined the DNA of the British Carry On films with that of the Naked Gun trilogy. *Conker's Bad Fur Day* is a cult classic, but there is one very important aspect of the game that people too often overlook. Following the brilliance of the introductory sequence that perfectly apes Kubrick's *A Clockwork Orange*, we are greeted with the visual of Conker's girlfriend Berri – a small, light-brown chipmunk in her debut appearance, now a taller, greyer, leggier version adorned with a pink sports bikini – doing aerobics with her headphones on. This is a crucial scene not only because it is the only real glimpse we get into Conker's life outside of the titular game that sends him on a madcap adventure full of movie spoofs and singing piles of poop, but also because in this scene we get a really good look at Berri's butt.

Berri's butt is the featured character of the scene. Yes, Conker is speaking over the footage as he drunkenly tries to explain via phone message why he won't be coming home until much later. However, we spend a good minute of the intro getting to gawk at her booty in all its blocky-textured glory, the only glimpse we get of the life he wants to save, meaning that this game might as well be structured entirely around her furry, round butt.

A recurring theme throughout the game is Conker wanting to get home and for things to return to normal. These brief clips of Berri touching her toes and doing handstands – all while the audience's view is quite intentionally centred on her backside – are all we have to show us what Conker is striving for, his ultimate goal to go home and be with his girlfriend. Berri's butt is literally the visual representation of Conker's 'good' fur day. Without it, there would be no innate desire for the player, as Conker, to find their way through the mazes, over the platforms and out of the intense, gag-riddled combat sequences. The player has to know that Berri's butt is waiting for Conker when he gets home.

The way *Conker's Bad Fur Day* ends – with the eponymous hero becoming the king, surrounded by loyal subjects yet realising how unsatisfying this all is – suggests that Conker would have rather just have a nice butt to squeeze than any of the riches or power he acquires.

Berri's butt is one of the most important butts in video games, acting as the catalyst for the N64's sole comedic adult adventure game, and should be heralded as such. It's a struggle to think of any other game where the MacGuffin was your partner's arse

MINECRAFT

🎮 Steve

While many of you may not know him by name, you almost certainly know him to look at. Steve is the name of the default male skin in *Minecraft*, one of the most popular video games ever released, in which players mine resources and use them to craft tools and structures with their friends.

Steve has an entirely flat and angular butt, which is unsurprising considering *Minecraft*'s whole world is made up of cubes. In most situations, having a butt made entirely of cubes and rectangles would be an issue, in that you wouldn't really be designed to work with any ergonomic seating or clothing, but in the world of *Minecraft* a rectangular butt is actually highly practical. Every chair in *Minecraft*, every doorway, every item of clothing, every staircase and bed, is perfectly designed to accommodate a rectangular frame, and this makes finding things that fit you comfortably a breeze. In a square world, you need a square butt to keep up.

DEAD RISING

Zombies

There are couple of key questions about zombie butts, so let's try to get to the bottom of them. The big question: do zombie butts poop?

It might seem like an odd thing to ask, but hear this out. Zombies eat brains, right? And presumably those brains have to go somewhere. Most zombie lore refers to zombies as having an eternal, insatiable hunger for brains, which means they're not eating a few brains and getting full – they keep going. But the brains they eat have to leave their body at some point, so that means zombie butts definitely have to poop. It's simple science.

Additionally, does a zombie butt get harder or softer the longer it's a member of the living dead? When a typical human body dies, it undergoes rigor mortis, whereby the muscles in the body solidify to the point that they cannot easily be moved. This doesn't appear to happen to zombies, because they are still able to walk around post-death, which would require working muscles.

With that in mind, the only real option is for them to decompose, which is a typical feature of many zombie designs. This means the muscle and fat and skin on the butt would probably soften up to the point of falling off, temporarily giving them a luxuriously soft butt before giving them a butt that drops piles of butt tissue. It's not appealing, but there's clearly a beautiful, brief moment before decomposition where it's probably a really nice kind of soft.

PORTAL 2

Chell

In the Portal games, you primarily play as Chell, a research subject trapped inside a deadly research facility with questionable safety procedures and a murderous lead scientist AI. While in the original *Portal* the character of Chell is a healthy young woman who appears to be in peak physical shape, neither Chell nor her butt appear as athletically toned when the player reaches the sequel, *Portal 2*.

The beginning of *Portal 2* features Chell trapped in a cryogenic suspension facility for an undisclosed amount of time. When this facility is operating correctly, Chell is woken up every fifty days in order to ensure she remains physically and mentally healthy, but this schedule quickly goes awry. We soon wake up from suspension to hear the following message: 'Good morning. You have been in suspension for nine... nine... nine... nine... nine... ni—'

Assuming that we finish saying this final nine, and no further nines, and that this is an accurate sequential count of the number of days she has been in suspension, Chell has been in suspension accidently for around 2,700 years without being woken for any wellness checks. If we decide to be a bit more forgiving, and assume the number was actually 999 and was simply repeated, this is still nearly three years in suspension rather than the planned two months.

When a body goes multiple years without moving, such as in a coma, even three years would be enough to see the muscles in the body, the glutes included, start to atrophy and waste away from disuse. It stands to reason that in *Portal 2*, Chell likely has incredibly weak muscles, including a very much withered butt.

So how do we manage not to notice this while playing? Well, jumpsuits do a great job of hiding reduced butt definition, and Chell's long-fall boots end up pulling a lot of weight so she can jump and land safely with minimal butt muscles to power those legs. Powerful springs are hiding the fact that her butt has wasted away.

🎮 GLaDOS

In the Portal games, GLaDOS is a gigantic, facility-wide robot AI who runs the testing facility that protagonist Chell is trapped in. While GLaDOS is an AI – basically a woman whose brain was shoved into a computer and ended up being corrupted by huge amounts of power – she does have a physical form, and as such she presumably has a butt.

So, where is her butt? Well, if you look at the whole facility she controls as being her body – as is the case during the first *Portal* and a lot of *Portal 2* – there's only one area that can be considered her behind, and that's the small, single-person-occupancy shed that Chell emerges from at the end of the second game.

Yes, Chell escapes Aperture Science, the facility that GlaDOS controls, at the end of the first *Portal*, but in that instance she escapes by ripping apart the station, exiting through a hole of her own creation never designed as an exit. The only time we see someone leave GLaDOS's Aperture facility the way they're intended to is at the end of *Portal 2*, where GLaDOS lifts Chell up a passageway to a small, designated exit. Chell and her companion Cube are expelled through a pipe leading to a small, metal shed in a remote cornfield. The pipe and its doorway act as the body's waste-expulsion system, with the shed surrounding this open-and-close passageway leading from the rest of the body and therefore taking the role of GLaDOS's butt.

GLaDOS's behind, then, is a rusty shed, that according to warning notices poses a high risk of electrical shock. That's not my idea of a fun butt.

THINGS I LEARNED FROM MARIO'S BUTT

DRAGON BALL Z

Guest Butt Critic
MasakoX

Lawrence Simpson, better known by his online handle MasakoX, is a founding member of Team Four Star, a group who create comedy abridged versions of anime series on YouTube. MasakoX voices Goku in *Dragon Ball Z Abridged*, a character who has been in more fighting video games than most, so he's particularly well qualified to analyse his character's butt.

Goku

Saiyan butts? Really? Yes, indeed. You might be surprised to hear that *Dragon Ball* is all about butts, but they're a lot more important to the series than you might think.

If you were a fan of the original *Dragon Ball* series, or games based upon it, the childhood incarnation of Son Goku often found himself naked, giving us a clear look at his butt and its many uses. Whether it be dunking for fish with his tail or exposing his derrière to taunt someone, Goku was never a character shy to reveal his cheeks. That sort of humour was very much creator Akira Toriyama's jam in the mid eighties. Juvenile? Yeah. Still funny? Also yeah!

Goku regularly exposing his cheeks was part of the original modus operandi for *Dragon Ball*: to make people laugh and not take the action too seriously. Goku is the epitome of that message.

Looking more at the form and function of his butt, a key part of its being present and correct in early content was his Saiyan tail. Used as a makeshift helicopter as well as for combat, the combo of Goku's powerful butt muscles and tail created a functionally varied and useful tool in his fighting arsenal.

As we move to more modern depictions of *Dragon Ball Z*, Goku's butt is less often directly visible, but it's not forgotten. There's just something about the muscular, Saiyan form that seems to lead to fantastic butts in adulthood. Saiyans are geared towards being tough and ready for action, which necessitates that every part of them has to be toned and strong, able to become more powerful on demand. Their butts are no exception.

In all his video-game appearances, Goku's butt has been a pinnacle of butt-design. Goku has fought untold challenges without ever staying dead, making his one of the most perfectly eternal butts in all of gaming.

CONAN EXILES

▣ Player Character

A book of butts wouldn't be complete without an entry on *Conan Exiles,* an open-world adventure-game set in the world of *Conan the Barbarian*. The game can be played in single-player or online in a shared persistent world, and most notably features a character creator where you can choose to run around with your butt exposed. No censorship, no requirement to wear underwear; you can just run around with your butt on display for all the rest of the game's online players to see in all its beauty.

Conan Exiles doesn't feature butt customisation, however, so there are only two human butts to look at. The masculine-coded butt is fitting for a hunter–gatherer scavenger, with a muscular frame covered with a layer of fat. It's a butt fit for running after prey or away from predators, but with enough fat stored on it to help retain energy in the lean, winter months and cold nights. It's a fuel source wrapped over a sprinting machine.

The feminine-coded butt is much the same – a muscular frame with some fat layered over. It's pretty large, looking likely to give a satisfying jiggle when running, but forms a beautiful pear shape.

Two absolutely beautiful butts that fit the context of the game and do not need hiding in any shape or form, and that I am constantly happy to share when playing online.

EXPLORING THE DETAILED MONSTER BUTTHOLES OF CONAN EXILES

Vebjørn Strømmen
Monster Butthole Designer

The human butts in *Conan Exiles* are gorgeous butts, praiseworthy for how unconcealed their appearance is in-game. However, there are also non-human butts in *Conan Exiles* that are also worthy of consideration. They were designed by monster and animal designer Vebjørn Strømmen, whose signature style, according to the game's PR agency, is 'giving all his creatures detailed buttholes'.

The opportunity of a conversation with Vebjørn wasn't one to turn down.

'The general start was a vertex error that QA reported, simply saying part of the design looked like a butthole. Instead of just fixing the mesh, we decided to paint the butthole in with more detail,' says Vebjørn of his origins designing highly-detailed monster buttholes for video games. According to Vebjørn, the initial vertex error actually occurred while designing for a different game, *Anarchy Online*, but it ended up being more than simply a one-off mistake. 'It was really fun taking that accident and adding detail to it, so I ended up adding a detailed butthole to a lot of my creature designs from that time on. It wasn't a staple in all my work – they're not present in *Age of Conan* – but I ended up returning to buttholes after a seven-year hiatus with *Conan Exiles*.'

Vebjørn seems to have a very clear memory of much his butthole-based journey, with a lot of milestone butts sticking firmly in his mind. 'The first animal in *Conan Exiles* that I gave a really detailed butthole was a rhino, and it just felt really right. To me, it just felt perfectly natural to put a few extra minutes into animal assholes. You always end up seeing them in nature programs; they're a part of the animal.

'I felt annoyed that *Conan Exiles* had a penis slider, but no sliders for the buttholes, so I slowly decided I was going to go balls-deep with my butthole creation, with incredible detail when it was appropriate for the specific monster. A great example, the Red Dragon, has a butthole so large that if you stand perfectly behind it, you can fit your characters head in it. It's the small things that make me smile when I work.'

Apparently, adding a little levity to a sometimes average day at work is a big part of this whole situation. It makes sense – designing a sheep is surely more workaday than designing a huge, elaborate, eldritch creature, and you've got to find that joy in your work where you can. 'It's a nice way to have a laugh when working on the more mundane animals. Not every animal is an interesting monster, and at least I can have a laugh when it comes to the butthole,' Vebjørn explains.

Vebjørn recounts that, while this started as a private joke for himself, it eventually became something of an entertaining talking point within the office. 'After a while, I found that I would get co-workers asking me, "But does it have a butthole?" when I told them about my new monsters. Once the team got in on the joke, it made it a lot easier for me to feel confident, so I just kept going with it.'

Vebjørn's creative process is apparently pretty simple. His animal butts are based on real-world research, and years of practice have given him a sixth sense for fictional anus designs. 'When it comes to just designing a run-of-the-mill real-world creature, I just image-search phrases like "tiger anus", and try to recreate what I find as accurately as possible. My reference folder at work certainly looks a little unusual at a glance. When trying to make an interesting monster butthole, I honestly just follow my heart. I've drawn enough monster buttholes at this point to know what I am doing.'

So how do other people tend to feel about Vebjørn's incredibly detailed work? While you might expect some pushback from players, if anything it seems as though most of the game's community want even more buttholes added. 'I'm pretty sure the guys I play with all notice the level of detail I put into the buttholes, particularly after we introduced pets. You can look at the pet calmly at your own leisure, from all angles, and get a good look at those cat butts.

'We do sometimes get complaints about my animal and monster buttholes, but not for the reasons you might think. We get queries like, "Why do most creatures get buttholes, while humans only get genitalia, but no butthole?" to which we have to explain it was an issue with space on textures.'

Learning about Vebjørn's butt-work is a truly eye-opening experience, due in no small part to the scarcity of game designers willing to be so candid about the butts they create, and who seem to love their work as much as Vebjørn does. *Conan Exiles* has some fantastic human butts, but the real story is that of a man who has made a name for himself making his office smile and laugh simply through the power of the butthole.

BANJO-KAZOOIE

▣ Kazooie

In the game *Banjo-Kazooie*, we experience the adventure of a bird and a bear who team up to save a young girl from the clutches of an evil witch. The primary playable character is Banjo the bear – the young girl's older brother – who runs around jumping, rolling and punching his way to save her.

Kazooie, the bird, plays more of a supporting role in the player's move-set, doing things like pecking, firing eggs and flying with Banjo on her back to go faster. This part of her move-set is the one of interest here.

A key fact about birds is that, in order for them to fly – which Kazooie is able to do – they have incredibly thin, fragile bones that are pretty much hollow and would in most cases be incapable of holding up a bear. For Kazooie to support the weight of a bear on her back and remain light enough to fly, she must be some kind of mutant bird with ultra-strong bones, including those in her butt. This adds up, because in order to fire those eggs at the speed they are fired, they would need to be shot out at enormous pressure, necessitating extremely strong, dense bones around the butt region. They must be made of something like adamantium.

BULLY

Jimmy Hopkins

In the 2006 video game *Bully*, you play fifteen-year-old ne'er-do-well Jimmy Hopkins, a young man who is dropped off at boarding school after getting kicked out of numerous schools, with one shot left before he ends up in juvenile detention. But we're not looking at Jimmy's butt here, we're talking about one of the primary ways he can interact with butts in-game – yes, it's time to learn about wedgies.

For the uninitiated, wedgies are a common schoolyard prank enacted by bullies, particularly as portrayed in media, where an individual comes up behind another student, grabs their underwear and deliberately pulls it as high up as possible, causing discomfort and even pain to the victim. In *Bully*, our playable character Jimmy can do these to any male student by walking up behind them, but at what cost?

When done lightly, a wedgie might not cause too much harm, but when done to extremes,

be that in hanging and atomic varieties, or just a particularly strong regular pull, a lot of real damage can be done. When men and boys (Jimmy's target) receive a wedgie, the result can be testicular or scrotal damage, which in some cases can be permanent and lead to other long-term complications. (In 2004, one ten-year-old boy who received a wedgie was injured so badly he had to have one of his testicles surgically reattached in an emergency surgery.) In terms of actual butts, while injuries to them are less common, they do occur, with symptoms ranging from bruising and friction burns to bleeding and cuts due to the sudden and extreme nature of fabric moving across the skin, particularly if the material bunches together in a small, narrow area such as between the buttocks.

So while Jimmy pulling wedgies in-game is treated as harmless enough, he's actually putting the health of his fellow students in seriously risky territory.

THINGS I LEARNED FROM MARIO'S BUTT

STREET FIGHTER

⊞ Poison

One of the few transgender characters in video games, Poison is a combatant in the Street Fighter series whose ever-changing attitude to showcasing her arse tells us a lot about how her body-positivity increases through the timeline of the games, and as she spends more time being out as a woman.

In early Street Fighter games, Poison wears more baggy, flowy clothing, disguising her body shape somewhat and making it tough for us to see her arse. This initial clothing choice will feel familiar as a coping tactic to many trans women, picking clothing that de-emphasises aspects of their body shape in order to more often be gendered correctly.

In later appearances in the series she wears more form-fitting clothing, often revealing more areas of skin – by having her legs on display, for example. This progression in outfits that show off her butt increasingly clearly mirrors the experiences of many trans women in their slow but steady rise in body confidence.

She gets more comfortable in her gender presentation, and less afraid of harassment for her body. She gradually shows off more and more of her arse post-transition. Also, much as we said with Birdo in Super Mario, oestrogen hormone replacement therapy makes your arse get huge, which is fun.

Chun-Li

Street Fighter's Chun-Li may spend most of her time in-game as a professional Tai Chi master, but if you go back to her early days she worked as an Interpol agent, hunting down international criminals across the globe.

Working for Interpol, Chun-Li had to travel a lot, and when a criminal was spotted she had to be prepared to run them down and catch them before they could get away. This required powerful legs capable of dashing off at a moment's notice.

With years of honing her leg muscles, and later a fighting style centred around her spinning kicks, the rest of Chun-Li's body needed to be able to keep up. Her arms were not naturally heavy enough to balance her kicks, hence her wearing heavy, spiked bracelets to help her lower- and upper-body momentum keep in sync.

This is also where Chun-Li's butt comes in. Since Chun-Li is artificially assisting her upper body to have the right momentum when spinning, she doesn't actually have much upper-body muscle doing that work. Her core has to be incredibly strong to make up for the difference in strength between her two different body regions, and it's her butt that ultimately does a lot of this work. Having developed into a toned, lean butt via both running and fighting, her arse clenches super-tight when she's kicking, in order to keep her body braced and turning as a single unit, allowing her to spin without snapping herself in two.

Chun-Li's butt is vital to her fighting style, then. Without it she'd constantly be twisting her stomach in painful and possibly damaging ways.

FATAL FURY

Guest Butt Critic
Slowbeef

Slowbeef, also known as Michael Sawyer, got his start on the Something Awful website forums back in 2007, where he is often credited as inventing the idea of *Let's Play* videos. In the decade or so since, he has been highly prolific on YouTube, creating and collaborating on numerous well known internet-gaming video series. Here he reviews a butt that many people will know for its owner's name perhaps more than its function.

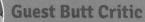 Khushnood Butt

'Oh, yes, I get it,' I'll presume some of you are saying. 'His name is Butt. Very clever. Next?' But, hold on, there's more to Khushnood's butt review than a name!

At first glance, it's a reasonable conclusion that Khushnood Butt is the product of an unfortunate translation – that his name was originally 'Batsu' or the like – but in fact, in the Japanese release of *Garou: Mark of the Wolves*, his name was Marco Rodriguez. This means someone translating the game for English speakers looked upon him and said, 'No, no, wait. This man is clearly named Butt.'

'Like Marco Butt? Or Pablo Butt?' I'm sure someone else asked in this scenario, which I just made up yet also surely happened.

'No, a cush nude butt, of course.'

'Did you say "Khushnood Butt"?'

And that's how it happened, if you ignore the logistical problems involved with such a conversation.

Butt is a man of many engimas. The game he's from, *Fatal Fury*, is a King of Fighters spin-off that's set in the 'near future', but since the game's release there have been many other King of Fighters games, themselves advancing the series' timeline. Butt has appeared in background cameos and endings of these games and spin-offs besides his own, as in *KoF: Maximum Impact 2*. Where exactly does he fit in the series? Or when? It's so mysterious that it leads me to recklessly claim that Butt transcended time itself to be before us.

Khushnood has a lot going for him in the personality department. 'Don't pity yourself so – I'll give you some pointers!' he says upon victory. See that? Even when defeating an opponent, Butt is the voice of encouragement. Followed up by another encouraging quote: 'Those burning eyes! I'll call you Butt Two.' Here, Butt even leaves open the possibility that there can be a Butt as wily and great as he... and it may even be you!

You see, there are all manner of butts, many attractive, but Butt is not about the butt you would want to see in the world.

Butt is about the Butt you should want to be in the world.

BAYONETTA

Bayonetta

In the Bayonetta games, the titular character is the product of a forbidden union. In the games' universe, reality was for aeons overseen by two distinct groups, the Umbra Witches and the Lumen Sages, each controlling half of existence and presiding over the powers of light and darkness. The two groups were forbidden to interact, as their combination would produce a power neither side could truly control.

Bayonetta's birth was the result of a relationship between an Umbra Witch and a Lumen Sage, and as a result she was born with incredible power, and the tools required to use that power as effectively as possible. In terms of how that power manifests, or how Bayonetta chooses to wield it, her butt is of vital importance.

Bayonetta has a traditionally perfect butt, likely a result of her very powerful lineage, and makes use of it to extend the ways she can use her powerful magical attacks. She's incredibly aware of her own curves, jiggle-physics and plump rump, and makes use of these traditionally appealing aspects of her design in order to distract enemies and catch them off guard with her attacks.

Bayonetta gloats, making sexual references as her clothes vanish, retracting into her hair, which forms powerful attacks. She knows her body is distracting her enemies from the giant demon wolf-face preparing to chew them in half; she uses it to her advantage – a body crafted by magically supercharged genetics – and loves every bit of attention her butt brings her, fully aware of its power as a tool of subterfuge.

GOD OF WAR

▣ Kratos

In the recently rebooted *God of War* on PS4, we follow the story of Kratos, the Greek god of war, who killed pretty much every Greek god there was, in revenge for being tricked into killing his own wife and daughter. This angry tale of vengeance is in strong contrast to where he begins his new adventure.

When *God of War* PS4 starts, Kratos has had a new kid, a son, as well as growing up himself and moving to settle down in core Norse-gods territory. He's a different man, but much of his essential character remains intact.

In the PS4 game, Kratos has aged considerably (both the passage of time and his lingering anger have taken their toll on his previously youthful appearance) but, as demonstrated by his in-game actions, he clearly has not let himself become lax despite his new domestic life as a father. Is his a house full of home comforts? No, it's solid-stone slabs and practical design choices. He's a rough-and-tumble man still, with a rough-and-tumble man's butt.

Kratos has a butt designed to survive hardships, a butt that will sit on a stone seat for hours and not complain once about discomfort. His ability to carry whole trees large distances in the opening of the game shows that his butt muscles are still powerful and extremely capable, even as he ages. Kratos wants to teach his son to be strong and tough, with no need for comforts to survive, and as such he leads by example, displaying a butt that is hardened to everything the world wants to throw its way.

SHENMUE

Ryo Hazuki

The original *Shenmue* is something of a cult-classic game, with those who love it often diehard fans. An open-world adventure game, *Shenmue* sees players take on the role of Ryo Hazuki, a martial arts master seeking revenge for the death of his father. While the game features role-play elements, brawling combat and minigames, its most notable feature is the day-and-night cycle, where certain events can only occur at certain in-game times.

The idea of the system is to get players to go explore side quests in between core game progression. However, in practice it led to players doing an awful lot of waiting around to be allowed to continue playing. This leads to an interesting divergence between the butts of the protagonist and the player. Ryo has a rock-hard, martial artist's arse, but the player likely does not. Considering the amount of sitting around on your arse needed to play this game, it's likely that most people playing end up with a little extra cushioning on their backsides just from sitting around doing nothing, waiting to carry on with the game.

Ryo's just lucky the programmers didn't develop the tech to have him, too, put on weight while he is hanging around, waiting for the shops to open.

BORDERLANDS

🎮 Ellie

When it comes to body-positive representation of larger ladies in video games, there are few examples out there better than Ellie, the plus-size mechanic from *Borderlands 2* and *3*.

Where most female video-game characters are designed to be, at largest, of average build, Ellie has a wide frame and limbs that make her hands and head look comparatively small, and wears clothing that is practical, first and foremost. But her size isn't something she feels any shame over. To the contrary, Ellie is incredibly proud of her body, and feels beautiful because of her size, not in spite of it. How do we know? Well, of course, because of her butt.

Ellie's butt is the location for one of the few bits of flair on her outfit – a single, solitary flower embroidered on one of her back pockets. Considering the rest of her outfit is so functional and plain – dungarees and a plain, sleeveless T-shirt – she clearly wants to draw attention to her butt. Her butt is functional, allowing ample cushioning from bruising when sitting on the ground doing repairs for hours on end. Her butt is both large enough to give a great handful to hold on to, and springy enough to make hugs comfortable as heck.

Ellie's butt-flower is the epitome of body-positivity at a larger size, and informs us greatly about how Ellie feels about herself as a character. Ellie has a lot of junk in the trunk, then, and she knows it. She's a fat girl and she's loving herself for it. She took one of her largest features and accentuated it with a flower, demonstrating to the player that while she is a big gal, she's not just content with that, but proud of it.

THINGS I LEARNED FROM MARIO'S BUTT

DIZZY

Dizzy

When initially asked to review the butt of Dizzy, a mascot platformer from the ZX Spectrum who is basically an egg with boxing gloves, I had a couple of challenges to overcome. Namely, I had to work out what part of him was his butt, and how to analyse the butt of a character with so little narrative lore.

Let's start with what we know about Dizzy. Dizzy as a character is designed to be an avatar for the player, deliberately kept simple by the designers so that anyone could connect with the character on his quest to save his friends and family: the Yolkfolk.

This makes a lot of sense when trying to identify the butt, because the simple, smooth, curved nature of the egg's lower rear-section can be interpreted in so many varied ways thanks to its lack of detail. By not specifically identifying one area of the egg as the butt, it means that any player, be their arse tiny or huge, can just assume that the percentage of that lower back-section that feels appropriate to them is the butt. Dizzy has no one set butt – his butt is whatever you feel it should be, and the deliberate simplified design makes that possible.

In terms of narrative critique, Dizzy's arse is defined by its fragility. Made of eggshell, one of the more fragile materials in our world, Dizzy is at constant threat of having his arse shatter if he sits down too hard or gets hit by the wrong enemy at the wrong time. Dizzy's butt is a butt we can all relate to – because don't we all sometimes feel a little fragile? Much like an eggshell butt, we are always at risk of damage if the wrong thing comes at the wrong time. It's hard not to be hurt in a world where we're all fragile, but Dizzy keeping his butt intact reminds us that we, too, can hold ourselves together and get through this with a smile on our faces.

Thank you to Pick-a-Butt supporter Christina Brien for selecting this character to appear in the book

Guest Butt Critic
Max Scoville

Video-game reviewer and on-camera personality at video game website IGN, Max Scoville has made a career of his personality-driven opinions, be it on video games or life in general. Appearing on such podcasts as *The Comedy Button* and *Weird Heat*, here Max discusses not just a single butt from a single game, but a series of butts from a series of games. Yes, you knew this was coming in a butts book: let's talk Metal Gear protagonist butts.

METAL GEAR SOLID SERIES

Solid Snake

It's all very well and good to jokingly compliment Solid Snake's behind, but have you ever stopped to think about the cultural significance of the Metal Gear protagonist's tactical-espionage arse cheeks?

The original *Metal Gear* introduced players to Solid Snake as well as the concept of a stealth game. While there's plenty of action to be had throughout the series, the defining mechanic of the Metal Gear franchise is the ability to sneak. And what are the best ways to sneak? Crouching, crawling, walking on tiptoe – you know, a variety of lower-body movements that'll give anyone a nicely toned derrière.

While the original *Metal Gear* had pretty rudimentary graphics, the box art suggested that Snake was inspired by a melange of action stars of the silver screen, including Kurt Russell, Mel Gibson and Michael Biehn, so there was never any doubt in the player's mind that the game's sneaky hero had the taut rump of a real Hollywood hunk.

In *Metal Gear 2: Solid Snake*, the ability to crouch was introduced, and Snake's haunches got quite a workout as he squatted and slithered his way through the many fences and vents of Zanzibar Land. However, it wasn't until the series leapt into 3D with *Metal Gear Solid* that we really began to grasp how nice Snake's arse might actually be. The crouching and crawling mechanics were improved, and tapping the PlayStation's 'X' button would make Snake perform squats rapidly, undoubtedly giving his glutes a 'solid' workout. Though the boxy graphics still didn't quite do his genetically engineered rear end justice, Snake's Sneaking Suit was introduced – a special, form-fitting tactical-espionage uniform designed primarily to quiet the wearer's movements, and secondarily to really show off that military-grade rear end.

Though strictly instructed to travel light on his covert mission into Shadow Moses, Snake smuggles in a whole pack of cigarettes. Allegedly, Snake does this by hiding them in his stomach, something made possible thanks to some fancy acid-suppressing shot he's given. But that's convoluted, even by Metal Gear standards. Let's be realistic: Snake probably hid his cigarettes up his arse.

The various incarnations of Snake's arse prior to *Metal Gear Solid 2: Sons of Liberty* were small potatoes. The hotly anticipated sequel brought the series to the PlayStation 2 and took full advantage of the new hardware's souped-up processing power. In addition to countless gameplay upgrades, groundbreaking enemy AI, a bucket of ice cubes that melted in real-time, and Olga Gurlukovich's nigh-photorealistic armpit stubble, *Sons of Liberty* also squeezed Snake into a brand-new, baby-blue Sneaking Suit, firmly (in more ways than one) establishing his sculpted downstairs Christmas hams as the best behind the video-game medium had ever seen.

Then, in one of the greatest surprise twists in video-game history, the player also relinquished control of Snake, instead taking on the role of Raiden, a flaxen-haired walking *Titanic* reference. Understandably, this upset some fans, but director Hideo Kojima's rationale was sound: one of the main reasons for the switch was to show Snake from another perspective. Presumably, he meant the rear perspective.

Solid Snake's sack full of fresh-baked bread wasn't the only prize patoot on display in *Sons of Liberty*, as Raiden famously had his clothing confiscated, forced to scamper and no-handedly cartwheel naked through one of the game's final areas.

Sons of Liberty concluded with a prescient mindfuck of a finale and an infuriating post-credits cliffhanger. Rather than follow up the ongoing adventures of simpering boy-ninja Raiden and his voluptuous, grizzled chaperone Solid Snake, the next Metal Gear game took a flying leap back in time.

Metal Gear Solid 3: Snake Eater shifted focus to a different Snake: Naked Snake, the American secret agent who would become the international warlord Big Boss, villain of the very first *Metal Gear*. Given that his DNA would be used to clone a veritable menagerie of super-soldier children, including Solid Snake, the Big Boss of *Metal Gear Solid 3* was nearly indistinguishable from the star of the previous games.

However, while this Cold-War-era tuchis might have been genetically identical to Solid Snake's sleek, twenty-first-century dumper, gone was the form-fitting Sneaking Suit, replaced by an entire wardrobe of relaxed-fit camo fatigues. If this wasn't bad enough, it was completely obscured from view by a canteen and a large, military-grade fanny pack (or 'bum bag' if you live in a part of the world where 'fanny' is slang for a woman's genitals). This might very well have been for the best, though.

As the title would suggest, one of the new mechanics in *Snake Eater* was the ability for Snake to eat all sorts of things he foraged in the woods, including wildlife. Even better, the food could spoil, and eating the wrong food (making Snake spin around in circles repeatedly) would cause him to projectile-vomit. With that in mind, maybe it's for the best that we didn't have a clear view of his dirt chute. Though it was a powerful console, the PlayStation 2 clearly wasn't ready for diarrhoea.

That would have to wait four long years for *Metal Gear Solid 4: Guns of the Patriots*, the hotly anticipated and incoherently numbered sequel to *Metal Gear Solid 2*, which featured a character named Johnny who constantly had diarrhoea, possibly due to nano-machines.

Thankfully, Solid Snake, who returned as the star of the entire game, didn't have diarrhoea (not visibly, anyway). Instead, he was suffering from a degenerative virus that made him age rapidly, as indicated by the fact that he'd grown a little moustache like someone's gun-loving grandpa might have worn. While his front side looked a bit worse for wear, his rear end never looked better.

Graphically, this was thanks to the PS3's cell-processing power running a brand new proprietary engine and the leap to high definition. Snake's rubbery new duds took most of the credit. His new OctoCamo suit allowed him to blend into his surroundings, but it also had artificial muscles built in, to account for Snake's geriatric physique. For all we know, Old Snake had saggy old Montgomery Burns' butt cheeks, but his new suit worked like a tactical cyberpunk pair of those Booty Pop women's undergarments advertised on late-night TV.

Sadly, *Metal Gear Solid 4* was the end of Solid Snake's story. *Snake Eater* got a sequel in the non-numbered PSP adventure *Metal Gear Solid: Peace Walker*, the story of which spilled over into *Metal Gear Solid V*. Sadly, *Metal Gear Solid V* was an unfinished masterpiece, with Kojima parting ways with publisher Konami, leaving behind the rights to his creation.

The future of the Metal Gear series is unclear, but it leaves behind a legacy of over a dozen titles, countless thrilling gameplay moments, a cast of dozens of colourful characters and two unforgettable butt cheeks: Solid Snake's.

Ironically, the snake, as an animal, doesn't really even have an arse. A real snake is just a head and then a body, and it sort of trails off, much like the plot of *Metal Gear Solid V*, or the current chapter of this book.

Metal Gear Solid

🎮 Meryl

The character Meryl in *Metal Gear Solid* has by far one of the most important butts in this entire book, because Meryl's butt is canonically vital to Solid Snake saving the world.

Meryl is a rookie soldier in *Metal Gear Solid* who is in possession of a key card our protagonist requires to prevent a missile launch. Now, how is Meryl's butt vital to this plot? Well, if it was less memorable, Snake would never have been able to find her and get that card.

Earlier in the game, Snake sees Meryl's butt while she's working out. Thankfully for Snake, her butt is very distinctive. Later, Meryl is disguised as a Genome soldier – a soldier injected with optimised genes to make them better soldiers – in a secret military base, and Snake has to work out which soldier is Meryl without alerting anyone to his presence. How does he manage? Well, by spotting her memorable butt.

Seriously, her memorable butt is so integral to the plot of *Metal Gear Solid*, there's an entire cutscene which takes place in a bathroom, where Meryl and Snake discuss her butt. This isn't extrapolation or assumption – we get a canon discussion of the fact Snake used her butt to find out which guard was her.

Johnny Sasaki

Another butt in the *Metal Gear* series with vital plot importance; let's talk less about the form, more about the function, of Johnny Sasaki's butt.

Our first proper look at the form of Johnny's butt is in the original *Metal Gear Solid*. He's the guard in charge of Meryl's prison cell, and when she escapes she strips him of his clothes to provide herself with a disguise, leaving him in just his underwear, butt pointed up in the air towards the camera.

Johnny Sasaki has irritable bowel syndrome, or IBS. A lifelong condition, it causes various symptoms in those with the condition, including bloating, constipation, diarrhoea and stomach pain. While his IBS is often played as a punchline in the series, it is actually a vitally important plot point in *Metal Gear Solid 4: Guns of the Patriots*. In *MGS 4*, all the soldiers have been injected with nano-machines which help suppress emotions, making them perfect soldiers, but also help maintain their general body-health. The fact that Johnny still has IBS is our first clue that Johnny never got injected with the nano-machines. He's afraid of needles, and even though it could provide a fictional future cure for his condition, he still refuses the injection.

The fact he hasn't had his IBS cured with nano-machines is the only reason he is able to save the day. Later in the game, an enemy named Psycho Mantis infiltrates the base, taking control of all the nano-machine-injected soldiers, including our hero, Solid Snake. Johnny is able to step up and free everyone from the villain's control because he never got his IBS cured with an injection of tiny robots. His IBS-having arse saves the day.

Metal Gear Solid 2

Guest Butt Critic
Greg Miller

Greg Miller is an internet personality who has made a name for himself sharing his opinions with the world. From his start as an editor and video host at video-game website IGN, to hosting his current YouTube and podcast project *Kinda Funny Games* alongside his co-hosting mates, not only does Greg know video games, he also knows how to enthusiastically explain why he loves them.

Greg is a big PlayStation gamer, making him just the right person to review one of PlayStation's most visible bare bottoms.

Raiden

If I'm being honest, I'm not sure I liked Raiden when I first saw him – until I saw his bare arse. Now, don't get me wrong; I wasn't one of those people who freaked out after the tanker in *Metal Gear Solid 2: Sons of Liberty* (you're reading a book about video-game butts so I assume you know that this is when the game switches after an hour or two from the series' protagonist Solid Snake to Raiden, a brand new character we had no idea we'd be playing for the rest of the experience) but I just didn't 'get' our platinum-haired runner-up for most of my first play-through. I mean, we were dropped into this new character and then given an experience that seemed so close to *Metal Gear Solid* but just fell short. They called me the same call-sign, I took orders from the same guy and I was taking down another group of weirdos as usual. I remember begging to see Snake again, and when I finally did, I was so confused as to why I was playing this whiny child and not the badass soldier I'd spent so many hours getting to know on my original PlayStation.

Then, Raiden got naked.

Stripped of his Sneaking Suit, Raiden has to wander dank and dark halls holding his genitals while the Colonel – the voice in his ear throughout this game and the voice in my ear throughout the original *Metal Gear Solid* – slowly unravels into madness and meta-reference about the fact that we're playing a video game. I was riveted – like, can't-take-your-eyes-off-the-screen, don't-know-what-to-believe riveted.

I make my living talking about video games, and for years I've talked about how playing *Metal Gear Solid* was the lightbulb moment for me, where I saw the potential of video games as a storytelling device. Sniper Wolf's final monologue and the discovery of the different endings: *Metal Gear Solid* was such a landmark game for me that I think it often overshadows this moment on the PlayStation 2.

Watching naked Raiden slowly learn that his entire life – the entire time I've spent with him – was a fabrication that made him very vulnerable. Not only was he stripped literally, but he was also stripped of everything he thought he knew. His purpose wasn't benevolent. His mentor wasn't real. His girlfriend was a plant. It was a masterstroke of storytelling that not only made me see him in a new light but also made me go back and replay the game over and over again to, sure, get every dog tag, but more importantly to see all the hints and cracks in the story I didn't notice before. That turning point made me love Raiden.

Metal Gear Solid might have been the game that made me understand where this medium was going, but *Metal Gear Solid 2: Sons of Liberty* was the game that made me understand what a goddamn genius Hideo Kojima was.

Hospital Butts

So, pretty big late-game spoilers here for *Metal Gear Solid V: The Phantom Pain*, but I have a theory that you can work out the game's biggest plot twist during the opening action sequence of the story. And, I seriously think butts are the key to working out the ending of *MGS V* incredibly early.

So, here's the big spoiler. While the beginning of *MGS V* tells players they're playing as Big Boss, they're actually just a soldier who has undergone plastic surgery and hypnotherapy in order to believe they are Big Boss, so that the real Big Boss can get on with secret missions undetected.

The game opens with a scene where the player, fake Big Boss, follows a man named Ishmael through a hospital, trying to escape while it's under attack. Ishmael is the true Big Boss, and I believe you can work this out from the game's opening scenes.

While Ishmael leads the player through the hospital, he is wearing an open-backed gown which exposes his buttocks to the player. The player is wearing trousers, but trousers which give a pretty good look at his butt. Here's my point: in the hospital-escape scene, you can see that Ishmael has an amazing, perfect, rock-hard, toned-to-high-heaven arse to die for, and the player-character has a decent, but pretty wide and flat, arse. The player doesn't have the arse of the world's greatest spy; his arse is a simply pale imitation of Ishmael's arse.

It should be clear to anyone paying attention to these arses that Ishmael is Big Boss. While the scientists were able give the soldier the face and memories of Big Boss, it was impossible to replicate that perfect arse. There's no faking an arse that good, and anyone who noticed that had the clues needed to solve the game's biggest mystery right at the start of the game.

THE SCIENCE THAT SUPPORTS SOLID SNAKE'S NERFED BUTT

A Super Smash Bros. Ultimate Critique

Alanah Pearce

Alanah Pearce is an on-camera personality, voice actor and gaming critic currently hosting shows on the comedy gaming YouTube channel Funhaus. Having previously worked at gaming outlets including IGN and produced numerous different types of gaming-related content over the years, she is also deeply dedicated to the science of gaming butts.

Here Alanah explores the butt of Snake from the Metal Gear games, and how it was done a true disservice with its reduction in *Super Smash Bros. Ultimate*.

At an E3 press conference in 2018, Nintendo announced that every character from every Smash Bros. game would be playable in *Smash Bros. Ultimate*, including Solid Snake, who was sadly missing from *Super Smash Bros. for Wii U*. The return of Snake even, excitingly, included the return of David Hayter, who voiced Solid Snake in almost every Metal Gear Solid game, and publicly shared his disappointment when he was replaced by Kiefer Sutherland in *Metal Gear Solid V: The Phantom Pain*. Everything seemed great

for long-time fans of Solid Snake and his iconically curvaceous butt, which was often complemented by the tight Lycra that is exclusively suited to his elite level of stealth espionage.

But tragedy struck the hearts of enthusiasts when, upon further inspection, it became clear that Snake's butt – one of the most significant culminations of the parts that create his alluring persona – had been flattened to less than a pancake. Nintendo had made the undignifying decision to both downsize and betray the bubble-esque shape of Snake's former buns, instead replacing them with something barely cupped by the tight fabric that caressed his comparatively overly muscular thighs. I could write paragraphs of prose about the disturbing betrayal this is to Snake's identity, and how truly offensive it is to have made him disproportionate, and while all of those complaints would be objectively valid, here I will instead criticise Nintendo with science.

By altering the perfection that was the dimensions of Snake's arse, the legendary mercenary would be rid of the various aerodynamic advantages that earned him such an esteemed title. If we apply the science found in the 2018 research paper 'Analysis and Qualitative Effects of Large Breasts on Aerodynamic Performance and Wake of a "Miss Kobayashi's Dragon Maid" Character',[1] which discusses the aerodynamic qualities of anime titties, we find that a flatter character model will incur a 4% maximum drag increase versus a more shapely body model, with an average of approximately 2% spanning velocities from 1 to 30 metres per second. More drag means less efficiency overall, so it would be harder for Snake to jump, and he would expel more energy when doing so, which is counter-productive in a video-game series that uses platforming and aerial navigation as a pillar of its gameplay.

As the dimensions of Snake's true butt and his butt as seen in Nintendo's false *Super Smash Bros. Ultimate* version are unknown, we are unable to confirm the exact change in velocity when compared to those of the aforementioned anime titties, but other laws still apply. Round shapes are inherently more aerodynamic than flat shapes because they 'smooth' airflow – this is a fact that influences the design of modern vehicles (where the process of rounding multiple panels, as well as often adding rear spoilers or side skirts, is known as 'coefficient of drag' or Cd).

In removing one of Snake's most Cd-friendly attributes, he is ailed by the same movement-drag as a vehicle, and is slowed significantly when moving left to right (especially on a 2D plane), as is the most common means of directional movement in *Super Smash Bros. Ultimate*. This is a disservice to Snake, but also a detriment to the enjoyment of gamers, who have been known to refer to movement drag as 'clunkiness' or 'heaviness', neither of which is broadly considered desirable in a fast-paced fighting game. By dragging Snake, Nintendo has potentially negatively impacted upon the overall enjoyment of *Super Smash Bros. Ultimate*.

In conclusion, not only did Nintendo's decision to all but remove Snake's butt indicate disregard for his character and the sense of identity he must tie to his previously proportionate physique, it also presented him with a significant aerodynamic disadvantage that indicates a lack of understanding of the core mechanics of their own game.

---

1 Analysis and Qualitative Effects of Large Breasts on Aerodynamic Performance and Wake of a 'Miss Kobayashi's Dragon Maid' Character, Rabino, N., Researchgate.net, January 2018

THINGS I LEARNED FROM MARIO'S BUTT

HITMAN

Agent 47

As a highly trained assassin, Agent 47's role in the Hitman games is to sneak into a variety of situations unnoticed, silently kill targets, and ideally get out before anyone knows what happened. As such, in order to be the best possible person at his job, there are a few things his butt needs to be.

In terms of appearance, Agent 47 needs an entirely forgettable butt. He frequently uses disguises to enter buildings undetected, so his butt has to pass for the butt of whichever person he's disguised as – but also be unmemorable after the encounter. He needs such a middling butt that you wouldn't notice anything wrong if he disguised himself as either a skinny or a fat target, and one you could never pick from a line-up. It's a tough line, but Agent 47 walks it perfectly.

Additionally, in terms of function, Agent 47 needs a butt that is disciplined and totally under his control at all times. A loud fart at the wrong moment could draw unwanted attention, and even a silent fart could be detected by someone with the right nose and lead to Agent 47 being found. He has to have total butt-related discipline, otherwise he would have been found out long before he got the chance to murder Sean Bean in that one elusive-target mission.

TEAM FORTRESS 2

Soldier

When a butt critic looks at the Soldier from *Team Fortress 2*, one thing is immediately obvious: where Solider should have a butt, he appears to have none. Just look at the back of his lower torso – he just has a flat frame with no visible butt. This isn't a *Team Fortress 2* design choice – other characters in the game have a butt, so what's the deal with Soldier?

First, it's important that we acknowledge that the soldier is aware of his lack of butt, and trying to disguise it. His long coat hides that section of his body, drawing attention elsewhere, which implies he doesn't want anyone asking where his butt actually is. He must have one – eating requires excreting – but what embarrassing place could his butt be?

There's only one answer. It's under his helmet.

Yes, that helmet that obscures his eyes: underneath it is a butt. It explains why he wears his helmet so low, which surely isn't beneficial for a soldier in combat. He would rather have his eyes visible, but he can't risk anyone seeing his forehead butt.

Seriously, you cannot deny there's a butt under that helmet, no matter how hard you try. This is now canon. Deal with it.

Guest Butt Critic
Justin McElroy

Justin McElroy is a prolific internet personality who has done everything from reviewing video games to creating an internet TV show with his brothers – and becoming one of the biggest names in podcasting.

Justin is currently best known for being a part of a number of popular podcasts, including comedy advice podcast *My Brother, My Brother and Me*, tabletop roleplay comedy podcast *The Adventure Zone* as well as *Sawbones*, *The Empty Bowl* and *Till Death Do Us Blart*.

Here Justin assesses gaming's most infamously Leonard-Nimoy-shaped fish.

SEAMAN

Seaman

Hello, everyone, and thank you for coming to my TED Talk. The question that... Umm, my clicker thing isn't working apparently, so if you could just load the first slide on my PowerPoint please? OK, great. So the question – ah, crap it's up there already isn't it? Well, yeah, so the question we're faced with today is: 'Does Seaman have a butt?'

The question has vexed gameologists for years and today I'd like to add my own lines to the ongoing conversation.

As you can see in this... next slide, please?... As you can see in these multiple oil paintings I've created, Seaman is like a golden fish with a man's face. He's got a voice, too, provided by Jeff Kramer of *Deadly Premonition* fame, but that's not germane to today's conversation. While Seaman does possess the face of an adult human, he lacks several other components traditionally associated with a human, such as left hand, right hand and belly button.

But what of butts? We know Seaman is pooping; this much is clear. The tank he resides in becomes clouded and he will hurl faeces at you upon command. But does one need a butt to create poop? I would suggest not.

I've created this lateral bisection of Seaman, with my best guesses of his intestinal inner-workings. On the left we – ah crap, I forgot to move the slides ahead... Could you just click through the... no, further, yeah, no I skipped all this... just... no, too far, go back one. Yes! OK. There.

So this is what Seaman would look like if you cut him in half, I think. As you can see, there is an alimentary canal through which faeces could travel, as well as an exit for those faeces. Rather than at the rear of the seaman, the faeces exit through the antenna-like rostrum at the top of his head. This rostrum, as an aside, is also used by Seaman to parasitically draw nutrition from Seaman's siblings and as a reproductive organ. If you're wondering why my diagram of his innards looks a bit like a game of Snakes and Ladders, it is hopefully clearer given my explanation.

Regardless, you could make a semantic case for the tip of the rostrum serving as Seaman's 'butthole'. But a butthole does not a butt make. Like all fish, Seaman lacks a gluteus maximus muscle, which is what we humans are referring to when we speak of butts. So one could fairly draw the conclusion that Seaman does not, in fact, have a butt.

But not so fast! To this point we have only discussed the second and most commonly thought of evolutionary form of Seaman: Gillman. It's easy to forget that Seaman was not just the human-face-fish-body hybrid depicted in the game's box art and limited marketing. At different phases of his life, Seaman is also a man-faced tadpole creature called a Mushroomer, a fish with rear legs called a Podfish and, most importantly for our purposes, Frogman: an amphibian with the face of a human and the body of a froglike creature.

In this next slide you'll see a stained glass window I fashioned for my Aunt Debbie's attic that includes a perfect 1-to-1 depiction of a Frogman. What's that you see nestled between those two rear legs?... Wrong... No... Wrong again... Why are none of you getting this? Right between the flipping legs! It's his: asssssszzzzzZZZZZzzz...zzzZZZZzzzz... aaaAAAAAAAAhhhhhhhhHHHHHHHHHHHaaaaaaAAAAAIIIIIIIIIEEEEEEE!!!!!!!!!

'... Hello, Dr Bromley. I'm sorry to call so late. It's Carl Sagan. I've... I've had the dream again.'

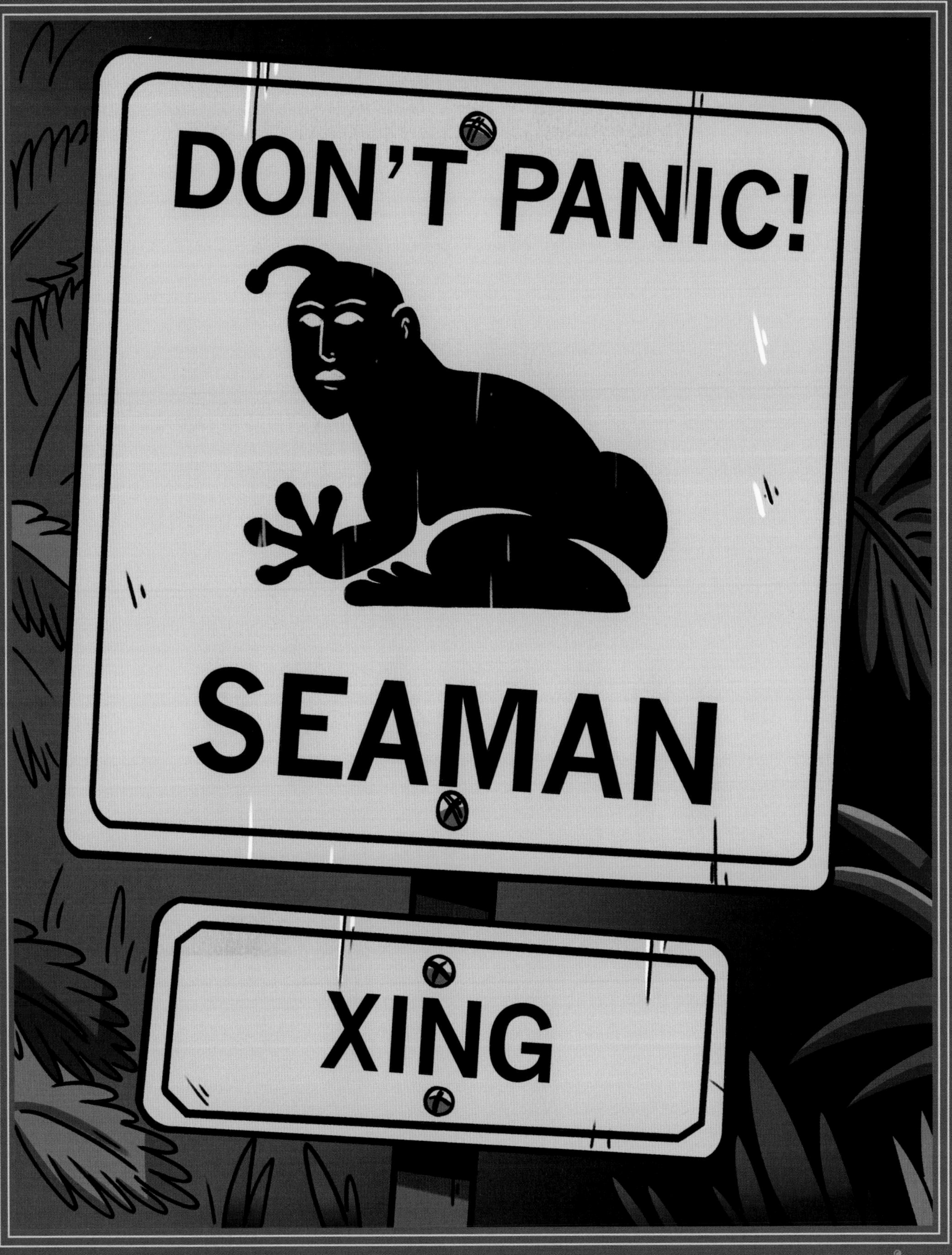
DON'T PANIC!
SEAMAN
XING

BATMAN: ARKHAM

Batman

Na-na-na-na-na-na-na-na Butt-man!

When it comes to Batman in the Arkham series of games, we have yet another male example of a phenomenon I like to call 'butt-glued Lycra'. Butt-glued Lycra is when a character wears an outfit that clings impossibly to every contour of the body in a way that it wouldn't unless it was glued into place. The butt is often a particularly notable example of this, because the depth of the crack would require you to get Lycra glued the whole way into the crevice to get the desired butt cheek definition.

As is often the case with cases of butt-glued Lycra, this would be particularly impractical for any kind of highly flexible movement, such as Batman's style of combat.

Now, if you can get a look at it, Batman has an amazing butt. It's taught, tight, muscular and just brimming with raw power. It's the butt you'd see on a statue of a Greek god, and that makes sense due to how much exercise he gets and the fact that physical strength is, like, half of his super power. (The other half, of course, is money.)

However, what's confusing about Batman's butt is the cape. The butt-glued Lycra would suggest he's incredibly proud of his butt and wants to show it off, but the cape would suggest he wants nobody to see his backside. This at first seems contradictory, but there's actually a good reason for it.

Batman is a superhero with a secret identity. He's super-proud of his butt, but if anyone gets too good a look at it for too long, they'll be able to recognise it as Bruce Wayne's. The Lycra is there because he loves his butt; the cape because he needs people to, at best, get a passing glimpse – it's good that people know Batman has a great arse but it's bad if they work out he has a specific great arse that they can pick from a line-up. Batman, it seems, wants the best of both worlds.

PAC-MAN

Pac-Man

When it comes to Pac-Man, and discussion of his butt, there's one simple question: when he dies, is Pac-Man eaten by his own butt?

One hypothesis is that, when injured, Pac-Man's butt turns inside out and kills the entire creature because it hasn't done its job. The mouth has failed to eat as required, so the arse eats as punishment.

The reason for believing this? Well, if we treat this spherical being as having straight-line digestion, with the mouth and arse as far apart in the main body cavity as possible to give the body time to digest those pellets, his arse would have to be the area directly on the opposite side of his mouth. When he dies, he turns inside out, starting with the area of his body we have established as the butt, vanishing before our very eyes.

MONSTER HUNTER

Palico

If you've ever played a Monster Hunter game, you'll be aware of the Palico, a race of small, bipedal cat-creatures who can in many of the games be recruited to assist you as companions. You're out there trying to take down a Rathalos; there's a battle-cat dressed in armour right by your side backing you up and offering support.

What's interesting about the butt of the Palico is the way it defies the typical laws of cat physiology, and what this suggests about these creatures' relationship to the humans they pair with. Put simply, cats can't stand up on their rear two legs for a number of reasons, but one of those reasons is the lack of defined buttocks. You need some muscles back there to bend, to support weight, and to keep the body in a position that is sustainable. The fact that this species of cat appears to have evolved to have enough of a set of buttocks to stand upright – after generations of our real-world cats deciding four legs is better – is probably connected to their symbiotic relationship with humans. The cats that could stand got given cool armour, and evolution then lead to those butt-having, rear-leg-standing cats becoming the ones directing the gene pool.

Also, Palico are just tall enough to come face to face with the player's backside. They are literally covering your arse.

DEVIL MAY CRY

Dante

Dante, one of the protagonists of the Devil May Cry series, is a Devil Hunter out for revenge. Born of a demon father and a human mother, he hunts down demons to seek retribution for the creatures that killed his mother and corrupted his older brother, Virgil.

Dante as a character is flippant and rude, the perfect example of a hero with a kiss-my-arse attitude. He is merciless in his quest for revenge, and while his lengthy trench coat prevents most direct viewing of his butt, we can surmise from context clues that his butt has to be pretty powerful. You need a strong, toned, utilitarian arse to power not only his strong physical attacks, but also to keep him constantly up on his feet, ever merciless, ever seeking that revenge that drives him. He can never stop his quest, and that demands an arse that won't quit.

As for exactly why he keeps his butt hidden under that lengthy trench coat, it may be a matter of pride, of trying to seem nonchalant. While he's full of quips and snide comments, he's the kind of character who likes to act aloof, too, as though he's never had to try to be this effortlessly cool.

However, if people could see his exemplary butt, they would know that he has had to work hard and go out of his way to do what he does, but the suggestion to others that he actually does care and make an effort would go against the image he presents to the world.

SHADOW OF THE COLOSSUS

The Second Colossus

Shadow of the Colossus is a game about the things we're willing to sacrifice and the prices we're willing to pay to get back that which has been lost to us. A moving game about committing evil acts for what is perceived to be a greater good, it sees the player defeating sixteen huge creatures known as colossi, with each one bringing the protagonist's beloved closer to revival.

The second Colossus in the game is a gigantic, four-legged beast, somewhat reminiscent of grazing cattle, that has to be defeated by shooting the soles of its feet in order to climb its fur and stab its weak points with your sword.

One of the weak points is its butt.

Yep, this gigantic, majestic creature that never deserved to be killed and was serving an important role in protecting the world, not only gets murdered by a tiny human but has the indignity of being murdered via a huge sword-wound to the butt. It really deserved better.

SONIC

Sonic the Hedgehog

If we know one thing about Sonic the Hedgehog, it's that he gotta go fast. That begs the question, is his butt designed for moving at speed? Is there a better butt-type out there for our blue, spikey friend?

Well, when we look at good runners' butts, they tend to have a few key factors in common. They're lean, toned and generally pretty small. They're a tiny package of powerful muscle designed purely to push the body to its limits

When we look at Sonic, allegedly the fastest thing alive when it comes to running on two legs, we see that his butt is so tiny it has almost vanished. This is not a total lack of butt – oh, far from it; in fact, Sonic's butt is so toned and dense that it has collapsed in on itself. Its own gravity has pulled it in and made it near invisible, which reduces drag and makes him more aerodynamic.

If Sonic's butt was tiny due to lack of muscle, it wouldn't be able to properly support Sonic's top-heavy design, so he has to have a tiny but incredibly powerful butt – the perfect butt for the one thing he wants to excel at. Those of us with visible butt cheeks can never dream of achieving such lofty running goals.

METROID

🎮 Samus Aran

Samus Aran, a space-faring bounty hunter and protagonist of numerous non-linear action-adventure games, was one of gaming's first notable female leads. However, the character isn't revealed to be female until after the original game is completed, and is left as a surprise to confuse the player's expectations. Sure, the game's producers kind of undercut their strong feminist message with the ability to 100% the original game to see Samus in her underwear, but her debut was still a big deal when it came to female characters in games.

The key question is, could Samus's butt have tipped off players early that she was a woman? If we look at the original pixel art from the NES *Metroid* game, Samus's armour generally doesn't give away much about her body shape, with her upper torso covered by a large, non-fitted breastplate. However, her butt is oddly pronounced, which one could argue might have signalled her as female.

We're obviously dealing here in broad generalisations, but oestrogen as a hormone tends to lead to specific types of body-fat distribution, one of which is putting on weight on the buttocks in ways that those experiencing primarily testosterone-based growth don't. Based on this, it stands to reason that if Samus had been through an oestrogen-led puberty, she might have a more pronounced butt, which would help explain the large size of her behind in the original NES game. It wouldn't have been definitive proof, but it's a possible sign players could have looked out for.

⊟ Arthur

Back in the eighties, I loved Capcom's spooky-shooty-platformer *Ghosts 'n Goblins*. It was one of the finest coin-guzzlers of the time, even if it was more brutally difficult than nailing a jelly to the ceiling.

The game was big news – it even garnered some notoriety after featuring in the Australian soap opera *Neighbours*, where whiny, teenage-audience-surrogate Todd somehow became addicted to it and stole money to feed his skeleton-zapping habit.

My strongest memory of the game isn't the weird monsters or the dubious English translation ('Take a key for coming in!'), but the Ugh and the Moon. Whilst those sound like names from a children's book, they actually both refer to actions taken by the game's bearded protagonist, Arthur. The Ugh is a jump straight up in the air, during which Arthur makes an amusing half-surprised-caveman-half-angry-monkey pose. The Moon, the focus of this review, occurs when he has climbed to the top of a ladder – he bends over, showing his arse to the camera and effectively mooning everyone watching. Additionally, one of the features of *Ghosts 'n Goblins* is that Arthur's armour flies off when he is hit by an enemy, leaving him running around in his underpants. When put all together, this means you can get a man in his pants to moon people on command, which to ten-year-old boys is the funniest thing in the entire world.

The sequel, *Ghouls 'n Ghosts*, doesn't disappoint either. Not only are the Ugh and the Moon still present, but Arthur now wears comedy white boxer shorts with red spots on. This adds 25% to the humour of telling someone, 'There's a message for you!' then getting Arthur to show his bum when they look at the screen. Plus, the competent Atari ST conversion allowed me to moon people in the comfort of my own home. (We do not speak of the belated Atari ST conversion of *Ghosts 'n Goblins*, which didn't allow you to stop on a ladder to Moon. It even had redrawn graphics that omitted the Ugh. Reprehensible.)

Looking back, I realise that getting Arthur to point his botty at people was an early example of having fun via improper gameplay – that is, using a game's mechanics to mess around in a way not originally intended by the developer. Over the years this has been refined into an art, especially with open-world games, which have become something of a sandbox for the player to muck about in. A perfect example is the later Just Cause games, where the official missions are a bit rubbish but you can have immense fun attaching loads of explosive barrels to a fighter jet and launching it into a communications tower.

So that's why, whenever I stumble on a YouTube video of something amazing – or ludicrous – somebody has

NIER: AUTOMATA

🎮 2B

In *Nier: Automata*, 2B is an android designed for battle. She's quiet, reserved and painfully focused on achieving her mission. She's driven to be efficient, powerful and agile, and her butt reflects this in every way.

Being an android, she has no need for physical muscles to move, including no need for a butt, but she has one regardless, and it's bouncy, perky and the perfect size for a good handful of buttock. While it may seem strange that a streamlined battle android even has a butt, 2B is aware that the butt's weight and size plays an important role in bipedal life forms' ability to walk upright, and recognises the speed and power benefits of an energy source and driving motor positioned right at the top of the legs.

2B is a no-nonsense android with a beautiful, purposeful, no-nonsense butt. She doesn't need a butt, but she respects the value of having one anyway.

SPLATOON

Inkling

With Nintendo being a fairly family-focused company, and the online shooter genre being popular but too violent for Nintendo to put its weight behind, it makes sense that Nintendo was the company who thought to make *Splatoon*.

The idea of *Splatoon* is that you play an Inkling, a creature which is part kid, part squid. You run around using weapons, guns included, to shoot colourful neon paint at the floor, painting the level more than the other team to win. Yes, you can shoot your enemies to defeat them, but that's not the focus, and it doesn't win you any points in the primary game-modes.

Of the two forms the Inklings can take, kid and squid, we're going to be focusing on the squid form, because the squid's butt has an important role to play in the gameplay of *Splatoon*. When playing as a kid, your weapons deplete your tank

of stored-up paint, which acts very much like a colourful form of squid ink. As humans cannot produce ink, the character has to turn into a squid and hide safely in puddles of the colourful goo to refill their tanks. While the implication is that the squid is sucking up the inky paint from the puddle on the floor, this is not how squids work, as proven by the fact that the pool the squid hides in never depletes. In the real world, the area of squid anatomy that produces ink, the ink sac, is situated just before the rectum, and the standard rectal-expulsion mechanisms are used when the squid expels ink.

So, yeah, when you turn into a Squid to fill up your tank, you're actually generating colourful secretions using a sac stationed directly next to your bum.

YO-KAI WATCH

▢ Cheeksqueek

For the uninitiated, Yo-kai Watch is a series of video games somewhat similar to Pokémon, but instead of collecting monsters you collect talkative ghosts. Each of these ghosts, or Yo-kai, is the spirit or embodiment of a particular part of existence, including such strange creatures as a poodle with a handsome man's face, or an egg with luscious pink hair and a romance gun, but there's only one Yo-kai that we need to talk about here.

Cheeksqueek is the spirit of butts – it's like a game developer out there somewhere knew this book would one day be written and created a character just for this moment.

Cheeksqueek has a bum for a face, but also a butt where a human would have a butt. He attacks his enemies by spewing out an orange gas from his butt-face that definitely doesn't represent flatulence. I mean, there's nothing else it could conceivably be, but the game doesn't ever acknowledge that, so I guess it's some other butt-based gas expulsion. This god of butts is a bit of harmless, silly fun. Cheeksqueek just wants the people of the world to remember that butts don't have to be sexualised, or serious, or shameful. Butts can just provide light-hearted entertainment, and sometimes that's enough.

DUKE NUKEM

Duke Nukem

Duke Nukem, the protagonist of the Duke Nukem series of action-packed shooter games, is the video-game industry's mascot for excessive and overt masculinity. Ultraconfident, aggressive, uncouth and hyper-masculine, it says everything about the character that in *Duke Nukem Forever* our hero's ego is so big and powerful it acts as a shield, literally deflecting bullets.

Duke Nukem is the kind of man who will pick up a turd from a toilet, throw it at the wall, laugh then shoot a corridor full of aliens while cracking puns. So does his butt, too, reflect that hyper-masculine personality?

While Duke himself is pretty muscular in all the areas of his body that he shows off, namely his abs and arms, his butt may actually be an area shamefully lacking in muscle. If you look at modern images of the man from behind, you'll notice that not only is the butt area of his jeans decidedly baggy, but he's also wearing suspenders to hold his jeans up. Those suspenders are vital, because while muscular to the max everywhere else, Duke's butt is too small to fill out and hold up a pair of men's jeans effectively.

My suspicion: Duke is overcompensating with the personality and bravado. He's acting like the epitome of super-strong macho-man so you won't stop and look closely enough to notice he has a tiny, weak butt hidden back there, failing to hold up his denim.

FINAL FANTASY XV

⊡ Noctis

When we first meet our protagonist, the young prince Noctis, in *Final Fantasy XV*, he is leaving home for the first time, on a road trip with his friends-cum-bodyguards in order to be married to the princess of a neighbouring nation.

The marriage is one negotiated by the higher royalty, a marriage made to form an alliance between the two nations. So what does this have to do with Noctis's butt? Simple – his butt is attractive and physically fit because it has to be. He has been raised to be a desirable royal, a royal capable of forming this alliance, and to be desirable by other nations he has to have a good butt.

A good butt is a sign of a prince who knows how to take care of himself. A physically fit butt shows he's a proactive king who's not afraid to get up and out there, helping his citizens in direct, actionable ways. A good butt shows he can take care of his public image and won't be an embarrassment to either nation once the alliance has been formed.

Additionally, have you seen those 'warp-strikes' Noctis does, where he throws himself and his sword up into the air and travels great distances in an instant? They must require some serious glutes to power them, and it's unlikely many of us have a good enough butt to do them.

Lastly, there is one final aspect of Noctis's butt to discuss, and that is what it tells us at the end of the game about the mechanics of magical crystals in the Final Fantasy universe. Bodies atrophy when left inactive for long periods of time, such as when people are in comas, if not regularly exercised by outside forces. You might assume Noctis's butt atrophied during his years spent frozen in time in a crystal, towards the end of *Final Fantasy XV*, but that warp-strike needs top-notch glutes, and he can still do the move after he reawakens. From this we know that the time statis crystal in the game not only allows Noctis to grow and age, but also keeps his muscles in full working order, ready for action when the right time comes.

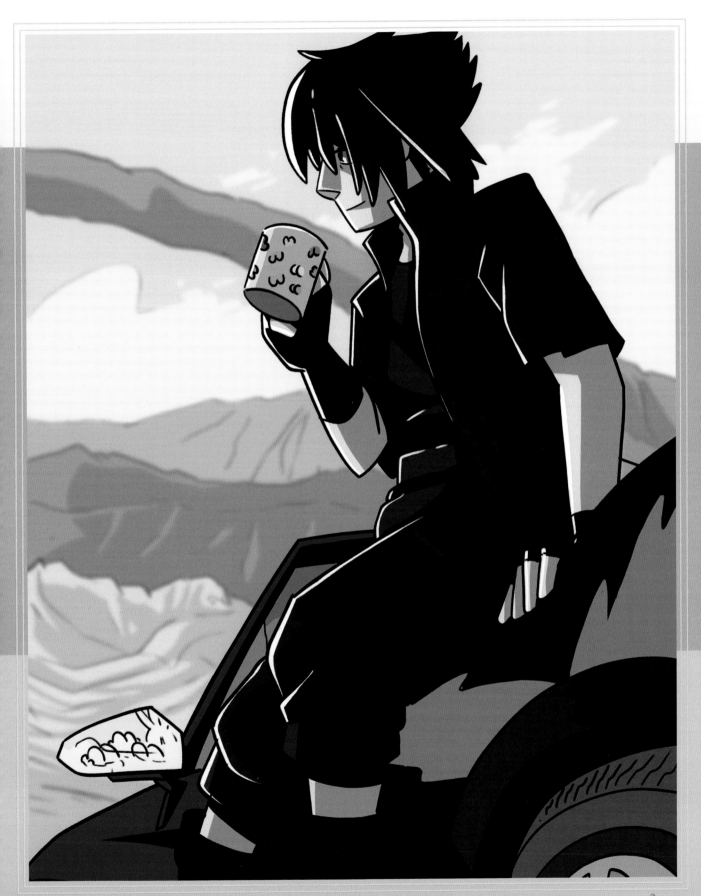

TONY HAWK'S PRO SKATER

Tony Hawk

When it comes to reviewing the butt of Tony Hawk, we have to bear in mind that Mr Hawk is both a video-game character and a real human being. What matters to us is the accuracy of his butt's representation in video games. How well do his first and last video-game butts hold up when compared to the real thing? As a reference point, real-world Tony Hawk's butt is muscular in form but has a layer of cushioning over it to protect from falls. (If you're reading this, Mr Hawk, hopefully this isn't too weird of an experience.)

In the original game, *Tony Hawk's Pro Skater*, Mr Hawk's butt is portrayed as a completely-flat-nothing of a butt. Not so much as a bump; it's angular, flat, and wouldn't even hold up his skater jeans. Not a great representation of a butt. By the time we get to *Tony Hawk's Pro Skater 5*, however, we get a much more accurate butt representation that accurately captures the muscular frame and the level of cushioning.

In short, skater butt tech has come on leaps and bounds over the decades, and while the original *Pro Skater* is a much better game to play in many regards, *Pro Skater 5* is where you go if you want good skater butt tech.

THE LAST OF US

Ellie

Ellie, one of the primary characters in The Last of Us series, is a young woman who is immune to a fungal infection that has ravaged the world, turning its victims into zombie-style monsters. The series' first game focuses on the efforts of Ellie, along with an older man named Joel, to reach a hospital on the other side of the country where it may be possible to use her to cure the infection.

In the original *The Last of Us*, Joel and Ellie do eventually reach the hospital, but Joel learns that creating a cure from Ellie will mean removing part of her brain, killing her in the process. He refuses to let this happen, takes Ellie away and lies to her, saying that by the time they arrived it was already discovered that her immunity couldn't lead to a cure.

But what would have happened if she had been killed to create a cure? Most cures for diseases are distributed as vaccine injections, and these are usually best done into areas of deep fatty tissue. Some doctors might do these injections into the stomach, but many do them in the buttocks. If Ellie had died to provide a cure, she would likely have been saving people from their butts outwards; she would very literally have been saving their arses.

Acknowledgements

Thank you so much, everyone, for reading and supporting *Things I Learned From Mario's Butt*, and for making this book possible. I hope you enjoyed reading it as much as I enjoyed creating it. Back in the mid-2010s I had the silly idea to review video-game butts as a way to do something silly and light-hearted that challenged me to find interesting observations in the seemingly mundane. The fact that this book now physically exists out in the world means a great deal to me.

I hope that now you've reached the end, you know just a little more about butts and just how vital they are to the art of video games. Hopefully you chuckled at least a few times, too.

About the Author

Laura Kate Dale is a full-time video-game critic. She has previously worked as News Editor for Kotaku UK and as UK Editor for Destructiod, started the website Let's Play Video Games, and has done freelance work for IGN, Polygon, Vice, the *Guardian*, and Rock Paper Shotgun. This is Laura's second published book, the first being a serious memoir about growing up at the intersection of being LGBT and living with autism, titled *Uncomfortable Labels*.

About the Illustrator

Zack Flavin is an artist based out of Los Angeles. His focus is visual development and storyboarding for TV and video games. He grew up playing Nintendo, marvelling at the pixely and polygonal butts before him, and doodling up worlds of his own imagination filled with butts.

Unbound is the world's first crowdfunding publisher, established in 2011.

We believe that wonderful things can happen when you clear a path for people who share a passion. That's why we've built a platform that brings together readers and authors to crowdfund books they believe in – and give fresh ideas that don't fit the traditional mould the chance they deserve.

This book is in your hands because readers made it possible. Everyone who pledged their support is listed below. Join them by visiting unbound.com and supporting a book today.

Artemis Aarø

Aaron :p

James Addis

Kyle Adkins

Mikko Ala-Korte

Alison Alessi

Gordon Alexander

Ilya Alexeeff

Eric Allen

Aluslaw

Justin Alvey

Marc Ambler

Allison Ancel

Maddie Andersen

Carson Anderson

Jen Anderson

Oscar Andreasson

Sam Andrews

Alexander Answine

Jussi Anttila

David Apple

Celeste Arkeat

Stacey Arkless

Henry Armstrong

Angie Arnold

Roberto A. Arteaga

Jared Arthur

Stuart Ashen

Cara Asmir

Audrey

Aarni Auerniitty

Brent Augustine

Jim Avery

Lena Avery

Anthony Avila

Kyle Ayres

Aaron Bailey

Josephine Baird

Richard Bairwell

Sahil Bajaj

Jeremy "GameBuddy" Baker

Michael Baker

Emma Balay-Wilson

Michael Bales

Michael Ball

Adam Barber

Brendan Barker

Cory Barlog

Austin Barnes

Max Baron

Lucas Basler

Brady Baszler

Gage Batchelder

Christopher Bates

Tom Battey

Amelia Beamish

Conrad Bebbington

Anja Bech

Jack Bell

Winter Belmont

Matt Benner

Nicholas "The Droog" Bennett

Kenny Benoit

Eli Berg-Maas

Tristan Berlet

Jared Berman

Daniel Bernard

Charr Berry

Mattias Bertilsson

Chris Birch

Kristian Bittner

Stefan Bittner

Alexander Blackburn Sizemore

Dustin Blackwell

Kevin Blaire

Sam Blanchard

Aaron Blawas

Jan Arthur Blomvik

Joshua Bock

David Boden

Shane Bodman

Jeff Bohannon

Larry Bolin

Arik Borstad

Connor Bourn

Klaus Boven

Tom Bowers

Lewis Bowman

Donovan Boyle

Becca Bradford

Jake Brady

Eli Brand

Clement Brasseur

Stian Bratsberg

Lucien Breitkopf

Ryan Bremner

Cara Bridge

Christina Brien

Jacob Brodersen

Dorian Broski

Cathryn Brown

Mark Brown

Nick Brown

Timothy Brown

Josh Bruce

Travis Bryant

Declan Buchan

Colin Bundervoet

Benjamin Burden

Erwin Burema

Jasper Burgers

Nicholas Burgess

Stacey Burghardt

James Burkhardt

Lazlo Burns

Ross Burton

Joseph Busby

Andrew Busch

Stephen Butchard

Teag Caiach

Eduardo Calderon

Wayne Caldwell

Donovan Campbell

Michael Campbell

Tom Canton

Gavin Carlo

Wick Carr

Jay Carriere

Matthew Casseday

Nadia Castle

Stephen Castro

Gianni Ceccarelli

Chai

Chris Challis

Ollie Chamberlain

Christopher Chandler

Elie Chauvet

Francisco Chavando

Ray Cheche

A cheeky patron

Lim Cheng Yi

Garrett Chester

Robert Chisholm

Chris Christie

Gaweł Ciepielewski

Stan Claassen

Johan Claesson

Andrew Clancy

Bob Clark

Jeff Clark

Daniel Clarke

Mathew Clayton

Chris Clegg

Keegan Clements-Housser

Matthew Clive

Dane Close

Katheryn Clow

David Cluxton

Rachel Co

Shelby Cobb

Wayne Cogan

Coie and Dave

Jenny Colby

Justin Cole

Jonathon Coles

Brandon Coley

Johan Colliander

Jennifer Collins

Natalie Collins

colons

David Comber

Comicopia
ReBecca Compton
David Congdon
Johannah Cooke
Patrick Cooley
Aaron Copi
Margaret Cosgrave
Stelian "The Grand Imperial
    S.T." Costin
Chris Cotter
Michael J Cotton
Andrew Cowie
Hannah Cox
Michael Craft
Ryne Craig
Shawn Craig
Katy Crigler
Magnus Criwall
Michael Crouch
Ryan Crowe
csg Chris
Mike Cunningham
Dan Currie
James Curry
CuteNCudlyToo
Andrew D'Alessandro
Amanda D'Andrea
Jenny Dale
Cameron Daley
Anna Dark
Christopher Davidson
Leth Davidson
Bryan Davie
Arwain Davies

Matthew Davies
Theresa Davis
Paul Davison
Matt Dawidowicz
Jules de Bellefeuille Defoy
Benjamin de Groot
Colin De Groote
Thomas De Man
Joseph De Maria
Kathryn Dean
Amanda Dearborn
Adam Deemer
Marjane Del Caro
Andrew "Ranneko" Delaney
Barnabé Delcambre
Daniël den Heijer
Stewart Denew
Heather Dery
Kieran Desmond
David Devlin
Patrick Devlin
Samuel Dixon
Joseph Doherty
Leonardo Domingues
Christian Dos Reis
Greg Downing
Daniella Olivia Doyle
Joseph Doyle
Kevin Drake
Jeran Dudley
Roger Duggan
Anthony Dumas
Amy Dunham
Aaron Dunn

Joshua Dunn
Robert Dunphy
Brad Durbin
Rob Durbin
Joseph Durczak
Larry Dycus
eat pant
Cat and Eric Eccleston
Jeff Edelstein
Derek Edmister
Pim Ehrelind
EikoandMog
Erik Elestedt
Dominick Elio
Benjamin Elkington
Emma Ellinson
Dominic Ellis
Jonathan Elvery
Charles Ener
Viktor Engholm
Brant Englestein
Melanie Enteman
Jona Enzinger
Eri
Adric Etheredge
Kenji Eva
James Evans
Kyle Evans
Richard Faith
Daniel Falsetta
Amy Farish
Kit Farmer
Christopher Farnsworth
Abigail Farrell

Danny Faulkner

Erol Fazliu

Jess Fedje

Declan Feehily

Edward Feeley

Emma Felgate

Paddy Fellows

Kade Neko Ferguson

Gabriel Ferrer

Finally Time!

Bret Finley

Matt Fischer

Thomas Fish

Gerald Flavin

Joe Fletcher

William Flotte

Fluff

Love from Fluff x

Jørgen "Indymonster"
    Weinwick Førde

Anthoni Fortier

Pia Frankton

Paul Fraser

Sarah Fredericks

Neil Freemantle

AJ Fry

Scott Fryatt

Tina Furchert

Alex Furze

William Gafford

D. M. Gallagher

Harry Gallagher

Dickson Gan

Robin Garbe

Oni Garlicki

Stephen Gaulin

Benjamin George

Seth Gerrits

Jennifer Gibson

Elise Sakura Gibson-Baker

Isaac Gifford

Harminder Gill

Jamie Gillespie

Ylva Gløersen

Jon Glover

Marian Gogolka

Tyler Golemo

Lars Golombek

Anton Golukhov

Carlos Gonzalez

Sergio Gonzalez

Peter Goodlad

Holly Goodman

Keegan Gordon

Kieran Gore

Rebecca Gorman

Sarah Granoff

Mathias Leonhard Graversen

Jack Gray

Renan Greca

Chad Green

Jessie Green

Kai Green

Martin Greenberg

Douglas Gregory

Randyn Gries

Nathan Griffin

Matthew Griffing

Adam Griffiths

Joakim Grønning

Kaja Grønseth

Tobias Gruetzmacher

Kally Gulliver

Kim Andre Gundersen

Valdemar Gustafsson

Nelson Guzman

Máté Gyenes

Thomas H

Brian Habets

Johannes Häggqvist

Morgan Hale

Thomas Hale

David Hall

Laura F Hall

Michael Hall

Rob Hallam

Neill Halpin

Russell Hamm

James Hammer

Robert Hanton

Michael Hardy

Benjamin Harkin

Carl Harris

James Harrison

David Hastings

Greg Haugen

Sybille Hauser-Raspe

John Haydon

Tanner and Kristen Haynes

Megan Heartilly

Erwin Heemsbergen

Philip Heidorn

Tom Heinan

Johannes Heise

Joseph Heller

David Heming

Otto Hemmi

Matthew Alan Hemphill

Leigh Henderson

Maick Hendrick

Peter Herbert

Andrew Hernandez

Benjamin Hester

Katie Hibberts

Anna Hickey

Jonathon Hickey

Jesse Hietala

Abigail Hill

Jesse Hill

Joy Hinshilwood

Martha Hipley

Ed Hoc

Anne Holland

Delia Hollenbeck

Athena Hollow

Dane Holloway

Neil Holmes

Maggy Hølvold

Oliver Hood

Becky Hopkins

Sam Hopper

Jonathan Horn

Daryl Hornsby

Isabella Horrigan

Matthew Howard

Harry Huckle

Christian Huffman

Daniel George Hughes

John Hughes

Jordan Hughes

Rachael Hulvey

Callum Hunt

Matt Hurtado

Jessica Hurtgen

Lizzie Huxley-Jones

Samuel Huylebroeck

iammatto

Jon Ijas

IlseMakesStuff

Carsten Immel

Rick Ingham

Mattias Inghe

Sean Ingram

Dax Jackson

Drew Jackson

Theis Søgaard Jacobsen

Bill Jahnel

Keladry Jane

Sam & Ren Jänkälä

Stephen Jeffrey

Arne 'S Jegers

Katherine Jenkins

Jaehoon Jeong

JM

JohnHQLD

Arran Johnson

Dakota Johnson

William Johnston

Austin Jones

Ewan Jones

Justin Jones

John Jordan

Isaac Joskowicz Jr

Ju Man Jack

Stephen Juby

Noah Judson

K.S.

Michał Kału⊠ny

Ohad Kanne

Natalie Kapur

Nayan Karanth

Alyssa Karol

Henry Kathman

Jenika Katz

Robert Katz

Seán Kearney

Ben Keatley

Max Kelley

Laura Kelly

Evan Kennedy

Casey Kern

Trevor Kerrick

Ammar Khalid

Dan Kieran

Robert Kinns

Elliott "Kip" Kipper

Edward Kirk

Kjersti og Aron

Tobias Klaus

Terra Kloepfer

Antonia Knoblich-Hirst

Sara Korupp

kozeni

John Kozlowski

Aria Kraft

Maxime Kraus

Thomas Krolikowski

Charles Krupp

Becky Kucera

Suman Kugadasan

Marek Kulasenski

Martin Kunert

Rasmus Künstlicher

Morgan L'Fey

Nicole LaChance

Petri Lahti (Neturi)

Callum Laird

Teemu Laitinen

Dimitrios Lakoumentas

Josiah Lambert

Holly Lane

Stephen Langdon

Billy LaPorta

Bodan Larkham

Chris Larmouth

Alex Larsen

David Larson

Stefan Latour

Thomas Layfield

Cameron Lazear

Chris Le Cras

François LeBlanc

Rachel LeComte

Derek Ledbetter

Jennifer Lee

Simon Lee

Frederik Lefevre

Yuvi Leger

Hannah Lewis

Tobias Lilja

Odin Linga

Chris Linneman

Jay Logan

Jonathon Logan

Tobias Logan

Sarah Lokay

Rob Longmire

Jessi Looney

Ant Loughlin

Keefer Lowe

Michael Lubert

Jose Miguel Vicente Luna

Joseph Luo

Ken Lutz

Michael Lynch

Rachel Lynch

Sean Lyons-Burke

Mark Lyster

Morgan M.

Holly Macdonald

Sophie Macfarlane

Jane Magnet

Jade Magona

Rick Mallen

Kayden Mallory

Doro Malsch

Rudy Manchego

Herb Mann

Jacob Marion

Jack Marks

Aaron Marnell-Fox

Ciara Marshall

Matthew Marshall

Alma Marstein

David Marteney

James Martin

Joshua Martin

Phillip Martin

Tomás Martin

Briana Martini

Charlie Mason

Pip Mason

Peter Mastrippolito

Luke Mavin

Jeremy Mayo

Luke Mayor

Stephen Mc Devitt

Lorcan Mc Garry-Hunt

Mike McCarthy

Sean McCarthy

Patrick McClard

Jeremy McCormick

Lloyd McCrossan

Patrick McCulloch

Nicholas McDonald

Russell McGaha

Ciaran McGarry

Nick McGlynn

Jo McGovern

Sean McIntosh

Scott McKie

Valerie Meek

Nick Mellish

Menel

Mabel Mensink

Mallory Merryman

Edward Meyerding

Martin Milde

Amy Miles

Milla

Carmilla Mina

Lena Mitchell

Matthew Mitchell

John Mitchinson

Matthias Mogensen

Geoffrey Moore

Paul Morgan

Robert Morrice

Jason Morris

Gareth Morrish

Thomas Mortimer

Kristen Muenz

Paul Muir

Kevin Murphy

Alea Myatt

Joshua Natzke

Carlo Navato

Brett Nemlander

Gustaf Nerström

Matt Nevins

Rob Newstead

Kiel Newton

Lozz Newton

Thien-An Nguyen

Brad Nicholls

Eirik Nielsen

Mark Nifong

Ákos Nikházy

Marcus Noble

Noble Arcade

Jarrett Noblitt

Joshua Noecker

Kim Novice

Ian Nowell

Ciarán "Sarky" O'Brien

Thordon O'Flannagain

Niamh O'Reilly

Jack and Kristina O'Connell

Chris Ogden

Jorge Olivares

Kevin Oliver

Matt Osborne

Anthony Pace

Sydney Pacione

Ben Paddock

Joshua Panepinto

Andi Storm Pape

Joe Parente

Dominique, Paris

Braden Parker

Jarno Parmonen

Jesus Parra Jr

Rachel 'BlueKitty' Parsons

Jay Patel

Nikesh Patel

Alyx Payge

Elizabeth Payment

Jacob Payne

Robin Payne

Alanah Pearce

William Pearcy

Fabrizio Pedrazzini

Aaron Pelavin

Enzo Perez

John Perry

Michael Peterson

Daniel Petree

Erik Pettersson & Johan
   Karlsson

Eleanor Peyreton

Bran Phillips-Lewis

Phive

Severin Pick

Michael Pihulic

Cesar Pinedo

Anthony Pirrotta

Aaron Pirwitz

J. Kyle Pittman

Chris Plaatjes

Estefa Plamenco

Wojciech Podgórni

Robert Poliseno

Justin Pollard

Ellis Pomirchy

Robert Popham

Owen Potts

Lauma Pret

LK Pridgeon

Stephen Punter

Denis Pyshev

Clair Quartz

Nicholas Quevedo

Nykholas Quinones

Sam Quirke

Gavi Raab

Charles Raffaele

Tiina Rajasalo

Cody Ralston

Thomas Ramey

Amy Ramshaw

Carly Randall

Alarik Rantala

Raptorbricks

Amanda Møller Rasmussen

Rasmus Ravantti

Gordon Ream

Matthew Reed

Keith Reid

Justin Renchen

Alexander Rennerfelt

Luke Retallic

Yesenia Reveles

Annabell Reynolds

Matt Reynolds

Paul M. Reynolds

Katy Richard & Jennifer Hodge

Neal Rideout

Thef Ridge

Skylar Ridgeway

Maik Riedlsperger

Barry Ring

Raynaldo Rivera

Ben Robbins

Daniel Roberts

Bede Robertson

Zane Robinson

Ed Robson

Hunter Rodda

Joan Rodriguez

Simone Rodriguez

Sander Roest

Andrew Rogan

Jarvellis Rogers

Danny Rollings

Ellen Rose

Chris Ross

Joe Ruscio

Cole Rush

Hannah Rutherford

Zoltán Ruzsik

Tim S

Ruky Saavedra

Jason Salomone

Jason Sandmeyer

Robert Sanford

Chris Sansburn

Bladimir Santamaria

Michael Sarber

Katy Sardeson-Coe

Keeley Saunders

Alice Savage

Eric Sayour

Ryan Scanlin

Adam Schafer

Ben Schlear

Sandro Schmid

Mark Schoon

Rachel & Marten Schulz

Becky Scott Fairley

Shane Sedgwick

John Selden

Grayson Semmens

Ian Semmens

Jacqueline Sessa

Jessica Sexton

Nick Seymour

Anya Shanahan

Quinn Sharon

Chris Sharpe

Kayleigh Sherer

Joseph Shields

Stephen Shiu

Ofer Shpigel

Blue Sicx

Finn Siegmund

Amanda Sievers

Alice Sigurgrímsdóttir

Harvey Simmons

John Simpson

Jaspal Singh

Kieran Singh

Robert Singleton

Mikko Sirén

James Sjökvist

Sarah Sjöstedt

Charles Skeavington

Julia Skinner

Gedi Skog

Michael Skov

Mandala Skye

Zoa Smalley

Vincent Smeraldo

Alex Smith

Cory Smith

Damon Smith

James Smith

Lindsey Smith

Matthew Smith
Peterjon Smith
Tess Smith
Ben Smooker
Robert Snader
Erlend Solbakken Nikolaisen
Marcus Soll
Emilia Sorri
Oliver Compton Southgate
Rob "Sedatus" Spakovsky
Nicholas Spangler
Amelia Sparke
Joe Spotts
Sarah Spruce
Squid
Sam Standen
Ben Stanfield
Gabrielle Stanley-Sims
Ian Staton
Stephen Staver
Matt Stecklow
Hamish Steele
Peter Stehrer
Egon Steiner
Anders Stensson
Travis Stever
Justin Stewart
Andy Stone
Edward Stone
Justin Stone
Amy Stonehouse
Emma Strange
Robert Street
Stephen Strome

Benjamin Stubbings
Timothy Stump
Jøran Svartsund
Matthew Swabb
John Szymanek
T.H.O.R. from S.W.E.D.E.N.
Michelle Tabor
John Tate
Taullo
Calvin Taylor
Patrick Taylor
Tomuki Taylor
Nicholas Terwoord
Paul Thacker
theKuehm
Nicholas Thetford
Devin Thompson
Matt Thorne
Josh "JustAHare" Thornton
Ewan Tibbetts
Corey Tindall
To the best rat in my life
Matt Toews
Marsha Tomarchio
Gareth Tomlinson
Becky Toothill
Guro Torget
Kristine Totten
Amy Tournier
Eric Townsend
Michael Trinh
Thomas Trycieki
Joshua Tucker
Mustafa Tungekar

Ashley Turner
Callum Turner
James Turner
Joe Turner
Alex Turnpenny
Twinkling82
Ilmari Vacklin
Jos van Baren
Anthoinette van der Hurk
Nathan van Doorn
Brian Van Meter
Timothy Vancrey
Ted VanHoeven
Ryan Vaughan
Jimmy Vega
Sami Veillard
Edgar Velasco
Francesca Vernals
Matthieu Versteeg
Pere Lluís Vidal
Kristina Viggers
Maggie Vincent
Antonio Vincentelli
Paul Vine
James Vogel
Daniel Voight
Christoph Voigt
Jenny Vollmöller
Rian Voß
Lily Vulcano
Reynard Vulpini
Millie Wadkin
Justin Wagman
Andrew Wagoner

Michael Wainwright

Damon L. Wakes

Elliot Walker

Viktor Wallén

Chris Walling

Kieran Walsh

Stephen Walsh

Abi Rose Ward

Andrew Ward

James Ward

Jonathan Wardil

Ashley Watts

Dean Watts

WearyWolf

Riley Webster

Marcus Wedin

Ann Weisz

Alex Wells

Sarah-Louise Wells

Rhea Welsh

Marvin Welter

Angie Wenham

Taylor Wesolowsky

Emily Wessels

Aaron Westover

Will Westwater

Timothy "KingIsaacLinksr" Wetzel

Travis Wheeler

Danny White

Cynthia Whitetail

Stijn Wieger van der Heide

Ryan Wiemeyer

Rowen Wiesner

Kristoffer Wiklund

Brock Wilbur

Olivander Wilde

Charm Wilke

Kenneth Will

Tom Williams

Jesse Williams-Fuller

Neil Williamson

Daniel Wilson

Patrick Wilson

Matthew Wilson-Krasnovitch

Daniel Winch

Braxton Winders

Josey Wingfield

Caspian Wisher

Julie Wittrock

Evan Wong

Yu Wong

Daniel Wood

Gabriel Wood

Daniel Woolley

Toshi Xyrho

Vivian Yamamoto

Larry Yellingenby

Almi Yeoman

Richard Yeung

Ash Young

Jeff Young

Michael Young

Zalno

Sam Zdanowicz

Conrad Zimmerman

Dominik Laura Zine

Robert Zomers

Rayne Zukas